For Sonny and Ian and David,
with the deepest gratitude.

COPYRIGHT © 2014 GREENMOXIE

WRITTEN BY NIKKI FOTHERINGHAM

Photography by Igor Yu
Illustrations by Benjamin Allison

DESIGNED AND PUBLISHED BY JIB STRATEGIC

ISBN: 978-0-9939954-0-8

First Edition

TABLE OF CONTENTS

HOW GREENMOXIE WAS BORN

I grew up in Africa, on the shores of the Indian Ocean. My childhood was spent barefoot and outside with my toes in the deeply rich, red soil and the thing I liked most was the animals; they were everywhere!

Monkeys visited my garden every day, and we'd catch chameleons and put them on Smartie boxes to see what color they would turn. There were great whites in the ocean, hippos in the river and an owl which lived at the bottom of the garden and once spent an entire evening on the back of a chair in the living room before swooping soundlessly out of the door through which it had entered.

As I got older, things changed. Garbage littered the once-pristine beaches, droughts and floods caused by climate change decimated crops and the great whites and hippos are hunted nearly to extinction. The owl is gone, although I can't say where.

If you think this is turning into the last five minutes of every nature documentary when they tell you all the cute little animals you've been watching for the last hour are about to die and it's all your fault, then you are wrong. You see, there is still hope for the natural spaces we have left and the animals who inhabit them. There is always hope.

But for us to save these last vestiges of nature, we can't just do less of the bad things; we need to fundamentally change the way we consume. That's what living a greener life truly means; it's simply choosing to live a life that is a decidedly more rewarding and healthy.

Love passionately, eat well, respect nature and visit her often, love animals of all sizes and be profoundly kind to each other. These are the tenants I live by.

There's an African proverb that says: "If you think you are too small to make a difference, you haven't spent a night with a mosquito." Each person can make a difference. You can make a difference to your planet, your country, your community or your backyard and together, we can change the world.

MY GREEN LIFE

Every month I do one green thing. Sometimes these changes are big, like giving up my car, and sometimes they're small like putting a recycling bin in my kitchen. Other times they can be really fun like making upcycled things for my home.

My challenge to you: choose just one thing from all the suggestions in this book to add to your green life every month. Living green doesn't mean 'doing without,' it means 'doing differently' and you will find your life more abundant and joyful for it.

WHY SHOULD I CHOOSE GREEN LIVING IN THE CITY?

The core tenants of sustainability are to save resources for future generations and because they have innate value. Every day, 146,357 people die and 353,015 people are born which shows just how rapidly our population is growing.

About 3.5 billion people currently live in cities and, by 2030, almost 60% of the world's population will live in an urban area. These urban areas account for only 2% of the land, but use 70% of its energy and produce 75% of the greenhouse gas emissions. We need to do more to make our cities environmentally friendly.

Living in an urban space can actually be good for the environment as it prevents urban sprawl and reduces transport distances while centralizing commerce. If we can work towards reduced consumption and greater sustainability, we can ensure that our urban lives have a less devastating effect on our environment.

YOU DON'T HAVE TO BE A HIPPIE AND OWN A GOAT

Well, owning a goat isn't a terrible idea, but you can make a significant contribution with small changes too. Consume less so that you can choose to spend more on organic food, meat that comes from an animal who has seen the sun and tasted grass, on products that are sustainably created and last longer, on homes that are energy efficient and on transport methods that are kinder to you and your environment.

Say no to the drive-thru, plastic cheese, disposable, breakable, built-in obsolescence of our consumer age and YES! to the real, to the authentic and to the natural.

You will feel better, you will be healthier, you will be stronger and you will know that you are living a fundamentally more authentic life. It's the little things that we are asking and if, every day, in every way you are just a little better, your small incremental victories will add up to something big. And if we all change together, we will create something really big; a revolution that will save us all.

Welcome to your abundant life, green warrior.

CHAPTER 1

THE LIVING ROOM

Consuming less means you don't need new furniture every year. When you do need a couch or a coffee table, consider fixing up an old one rather than buying new furniture. Not only will you save an old couch from the landfill, but it will have off-gassed many of the harmful chemicals that were used in the manufacturing process. You can also upcycle already manufactured items and re-purpose them for use in your home.

PAPER MACHE UNICORN HEAD

…or deer, or moose, or gazelle, or giraffe or…

Mount this over your fireplace for an upcycled cottage feel. It's easy to make and you can use recycled materials too.

WHAT YOU NEED		
chicken wire	gloves	pliers
flour	water	salt
old phone books or newspapers		

INSTRUCTIONS

1) Use the chicken wire to shape the beast's head. Wear gloves to avoid having to get a tetanus shot. Lay some old newspapers down and place your chicken-wire frame on top. Cut the rest of the newspaper into strips. In a bowl, mix the flour and salt with enough water so that it is the consistency of pancake dough. Dip the strips of newspaper into the flour mixture and lay them down on the wire frame. You will have to leave one side to dry before turning it over to do the other side.

2) I recommend completing several layers (I usually do five) and then sanding the shape with a fine grit sandpaper. This step is optional, but it does give it a very smooth finish.

3) Paint your unicorn and hang it on the wall.

BATHTUB COUCH   OVERLEAF

BATHTUB COUCH

Bathtubs make surprisingly comfortable couches. After all, they were meant for lounging in. If you can dig up an old claw-foot cast-iron tub, even better! All you really need to do is cut one side off and give it a lick of paint.

WHAT YOU NEED				
marker		angle grinder		protective gloves
protective goggles	mask		VOC-free paint	sandpaper

INSTRUCTIONS

1) Wear the gloves, mask and goggles at all times. Since you want to remove one side of the tub, use the marker to draw a line for cutting along the bottom and side of your tub.
2) Use a 4.5-inch cut-off wheel on an angle grinder to cut your tub. This puts tremendous strain on the grinder, so stop from time to time to ensure that you don't burn out the motor.
3) Sand the edges of the cut and any rusted areas on your tub.
4) Paint with a suitable VOC-free paint and allow to dry.
5) Decorate with cushions for added comfort and pizzazz.

Note: Place newspaper under the tub when cutting or make sure you sweep up all the iron filings. If they are left on the ground and get wet, they will rust.

Minimize the amount of watering and pest control by planting native plant species which are accustomed to local conditions.

BOTTLE TERRARIUMS

Any bottle or glass container can be turned into a terrarium. Just add soil and plants. You can get into hard-to-reach places with chop sticks or make a hook with some wire and use as a planting tool. Terrariums need sunlight and water (not too much!) and work best with plants that enjoy a tropical atmosphere.

OLD TV PET BED

Old TV's and desktop computers (15-inch screens or bigger) make great beds for dogs and cats who both like enclosed living quarters. Simply remove the back of the appliance and everything inside taking care not to damage old TV tubes which contain hazardous materials.

Also note that the capacitors of TVs and monitors can hold a charge for months and it's possible to shock yourself. If you are concerned about hazardous materials and getting shocked, consider asking a technician to clear out the TV or monitor for you. Once your TV or monitor is down to the shell, you can paint it with VOC-free paint.

Use newspaper to line the bottom of the shell and trim it to fit snugly. This will be the pattern you will use to cut a piece of foam to fit your new pet bed. You can cover the foam with fabric that matches your brilliant paint job.

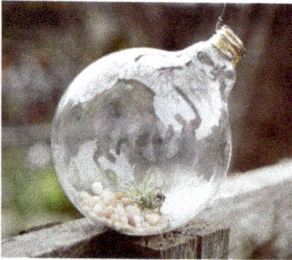

LIGHT BULB VASES

When I recently switched out my light bulbs, I was hesitant to throw away the incandescent ones. I realized I had developed a strange fondness for them and was lax to toss them out, so we turned them into vases which reflect the light brilliantly and look lovely hanging in my window.

WHAT YOU NEED			
gloves	hacksaw	light bulbs	needle-nose pliers
glue gun	metal file	metal washer	wire

INSTRUCTIONS

1) Carefully cut the metal top off the light bulb with a hacksaw. Use a needle-nose pliers to remove the filaments from inside of the bulb Wear gloves and be careful not to break the glass.

2) Use a metal file to smooth the jagged metal edge so that there is nothing that will stab you in the finger.

3) Use a glue gun to secure a metal washer onto the top of the vase to finish it off.

4) Wrap a small length of wire around the metal top of the vase. Twist it together (decoratively) at the back and make a loop at the top.

5) Screw a hook into your window frame and hang.

Your dryer uses more energy than most other home appliances. Use your dryer as a last resort and dry your clothes on the line when possible.

BOOK BOX

Is that an old edition of Finnegan's Wake on your bookshelf or a dashingly clever hiding place? Transform an old book into a perfect gift box or hiding place for your extra special goodies.

WHAT YOU NEED		
old hardcover book	pencil	ruler
white glue	paint brush	Xacto knife

INSTRUCTIONS

1) Open the book about half way through the pages. Hold the top half of the book and ensure that the spine is straight so that the bottom pages are sitting flush with each other. Use the pencil and ruler to draw a rectangle in the middle of the page, leaving a 2-inch border around the edges. If you are creating the book box for a specific item, you can lay the item on the page and trace around it.

2) Now use the ruler and the Xacto knife to cut along your lines to make a hole in the middle of the book. Discard the rectangular paper cut outs (or use them for origami).

3) Place the ruler into the center of the book before closing it so that you don't glue the pages from the top half and bottom half together.

4) Use the paint brush to paint the glue on all three sides of the pages so that they will be glued together. Leave to dry. Remove the ruler and you will have the perfect book box!

RECORD BOWLS   ↑

If you have old LPs lying around that you don't listen to or that are too scratched to play, you can make groovy record bowls in no time at all. Records make strong, durable bowls; simply pop your record into an oven set to 220°F or 100°C for 3-5 minutes. The bowl will be pliable so you can shape it any way you want. Don't like the shape of your bowl? Just pop it back into the oven and reshape.

THE KITCHEN

The kitchen is the heart of every home and our heart beats green.
Here are some great ideas and recipes for a healthier home.

MAKE YOUR OWN CHEESE

Making cheese is far easier than you think. Even hard cheeses require only a few items that you can buy from a health food store. We're going to make some soft cheese that requires no special ingredients (like rennet) and no special equipment. It's the best thing since, well… sliced cheese!

WHAT YOU NEED	
8 1/2 cups whole milk (you can use 2%)	1/2 cup vinegar
1/8 tsp. salt	cooking thermometer
colander	dish towel or cheesecloth

INSTRUCTIONS

1) Heat 8 cups of milk over a medium heat until it reaches a temperature of 120°F (49°C). Set ½ cup aside.
2) Remove from heat and slowly stir in the vinegar.
3) Your milk will start to curdle. Put the lid on the pot and leave it to cool for 30 minutes.
4) Line a colander with a clean dish towel or cheesecloth.
5) Pour the milk mixture into the colander. Rinse really well under cold water to get all the vinegar out.
6) Gather up the cloth and gently squeeze out any liquids.
7) Put your curds in a bowl and add the ½ cup milk and salt (add more milk if it seems dry and salt to taste). Mix well.
8) Enjoy your curd nerds!

MAKE YOUR OWN YOGURT

OK, this stuff is really good. Sure, you need store-bought yogurt to begin, but once you start making your own, you'll never go back!

WHAT YOU NEED		
8 cups whole milk (you can use 2%)		1/2 cup plain yogurt with live cultures
large pot or Dutch oven		cooking thermometer
small bowl	whisk	2 towels

INSTRUCTIONS

1) Heat the milk over a medium heat to 200°F (93°C), stirring gently. Let the milk cool to 115°F (46°C).
2) Heat your oven to 115°F (46°C). Pour a cup of milk into the small bowl, and whisk in the yogurt until smooth.
3) Pour the yogurt mixture back into the milk and stir. Put a lid on the pot or Dutch oven, wrap it in the towels and place it in the oven.
4) Turn the oven off. Leave to set for 4 hours.
5) Check on your yogurt to see if it's the right consistency.
6) If you like it thicker, let it sit for closer to 6 hours. You can use a cup of this yogurt to make the next batch so you never have to buy yogurt again.

DIY JAR SPROUTS

You can make your own sprouts in a jar with a metal or plastic lid in three to four days. Once you have made the sprouting jar, you can reuse it as often as you like, making sure to clean it well between crops.

WHAT YOU NEED			
glass jar	lid	nail and hammer	1 1/3 cup sprouts

INSTRUCTIONS

1) Use the nail and hammer to punch holes in the lid of the jar. There should be at least six or seven holes in a 250ml (8.45 oz.) jar lid.
2) Put the lentils in the jar and rinse with fresh water. Add 2 cups of water and put the lid on the jar. Leave in a warm, bright place like a windowsill or counter top.
3) After 24 hours, turn the jar upside down over the sink so all the water drains.
4) Add a little water to rinse the sprouts about three to four times a day. Drain the water each time and place the jar back on the windowsill or counter.
5) After three or four days you will have edible sprouts.

AIR FRESHENERS

Love the dulcet scent of pine which makes you feel like you're in the woods, or the delicate fragrance of vanilla and orange blossom which transforms your house into a bakery-orchid?

I have always enjoyed the ease with which an air freshener can mask the odor of dog and old sock. But air fresheners are just chemical concoctions which we use to mask our already unsanitary indoor atmosphere. The most pressing problem with air fresheners is that they don't freshen air.

The EPA claims that indoor air is usually 2 to 5 times more polluted than outdoor air which is pretty disturbing in itself, but when we add a bunch of chemicals to make the place smell better, we exacerbate the problem. Here are some easy DIY fresheners that will leave your home smelling great.

TIP Done with your book? Set it free by leaving it outside on a park bench, in a station or on the curb with a note inviting the next person to read it. You can register the book at www.bookcrossing.com if you want to see where it ends up or calculate how many trees you save as the book finds its way across the globe. You can also write a note on the front page that others can add to as they pass your book on.

VODKA AIR FRESHENER

Wait… what? Actually vodka is a great way to clean and freshen your air. The alcohol in vodka kills germs as it cleans.

WHAT YOU NEED	
cup of water	2 tablespoons of non-flavored vodka
spray bottle	add a couple of drops of essential oil if you want to add a nice fragrance

INSTRUCTIONS

Mix the ingredients in the bottle and spray around your home.

CITRUS FRESHENER

If you have just enjoyed an orange, drop the peels into a pot of hot water and simmer gently on the stove to infuse your home with a delicious citrus smell. This is an especially great idea if your indoor air is a little dry. You can also use this recipe:

WHAT YOU NEED	
small pot filled 2/3 with water	2 tsp. vanilla essence
3 sprigs rosemary	1 lemon (sliced)

INSTRUCTIONS

Bring to the boil and then turn the heat down to a very gentle simmer. You can keep this going for up to two days, adding water as required for a lovely fresh spring-scented home.

BAKING SODA AIR FRESHENER

Baking soda does a great job of soaking up bad smells. You can sprinkle it on your carpets, put some in your fridge and throw it in the bottom of your garbage bin. You can also add some essential oils so that it absorbs bad smells and releases good ones for the double sweet-smelling whammy.

WHAT YOU NEED			
small Mason jar	pencil	scissors	pin
1/2 cup baking soda	gift wrap	10 drops essential oil of your choice	

INSTRUCTIONS

Pour the baking soda into the jar and drip the essential oil over it. Place the Mason jar screw top onto the gift wrap and trace around it. Cut out the circle and poke holes in it with the pin. Cover the jar with the gift wrap circle and screw on the top.

TIP Stay on the path when hiking in natural areas to mitigate soil erosion and prevent the squishing of plants and insects.

TIP How toxic are your tootsies? Many nail lacquers contain the "toxic-trio" of chemicals. These are Toluene, Dibutyl Phthalate, and Formaldehyde. Opt for lacquers that are 'three-free' or water-based to ensure that your mani-pedi is safe.

SOOTHING LAVENDER AIR FRESHENER

This recipe combines lavender and chamomile which both boast calming properties; they disinfect while soothing the soul. This is a great freshener to use if you are sending the family off to sleep or to elevate mood. If you are planning an all-night rave, this is not the air freshener for you; opt for the citrus freshener instead.

WHAT YOU NEED		
2 cups distilled water	1 tsp. baking soda	spray bottle
10 drops essential lavender oil		10 drops essential chamomile oil

INSTRUCTIONS

Mix ingredients together in the spray bottle and spritz your blues away.

TIP Save energy by reducing the temperature of your hot water heater to 140°F (60°C).

TIP Avoid constantly buying younger kids new toys by putting some toys away for a couple of months and then reintroducing them. If your younger kids get a huge pile of toys over holidays and birthdays, squirrel some away for a rainy day.

FURNITURE POLISH

Commercial furniture polishes are made from petroleum distillates which contain harmful chemicals. You can buy green products that are made with natural ingredients like beeswax or make your own!

WHAT YOU NEED	
1/2 cup olive oil	1/4 cup distilled white vinegar
1 tsp. lemon juice	

INSTRUCTIONS

Mix in a plastic container. Apply with a soft cloth and buff for a shiny finish. Store in the fridge for future use.

TIP Eat locally! It's fun to try different cuisine, locally grown food will have a lower carbon footprint and you will be supporting local farmers.

TIP Use crayons made from soya bean oil rather than from paraffin wax (a petroleum derivative). The same goes for markers; use the water-based ones rather than the smelly chemical variety.

SILVER POLISH

Spruce up your silverware without using harmful chemical cleaners. Use this easy method to get your flatware shining in no time.

WHAT YOU NEED			
bowl	foil	salt	baking soda

INSTRUCTIONS

Line your bowl with foil and sprinkle a tablespoon of salt and a tablespoon of baking soda on the bottom. Lay the silverware in the bowl and fill with warm water. The tarnish will migrate to the foil, leaving your flatware sparkling. Buff with a soft cloth.

Good news! If you use an energy and water-efficient model and only do a wash when its full, using a dishwasher is actually more environmentally friendly than hand-washing your dishes.

9 FRUITS AND VEGGIES YOU ONLY NEED TO BUY ONCE

Do you love the idea of harvesting fresh herbs, fruit and vegetables right in your own home? Here are nine foods that you can buy once and then regrow.

An interior designer friend once told me that you should have a living thing in every room and I so have endeavored to fill my home with plants, many of which are edible. Plants not only help to reduce stress, elevate mood and reduce blood pressure, they are also invaluable in keeping your indoor air clean.

1) GREEN ONIONS

You can just pop the white ends of the green onions in a glass or vase filled with water and chop the tops off whenever you need them; they will keep growing back. Plant them for even faster regrowth.

2) LEEKS

These work in the same way as green onions. Just chop off the green leaves and place the fleshy white bottoms in water.

3) CELERY

Chop the bottom off the celery and pop it into a bowl of warm water (the water should just cover the bottom of the plant) and then leave it in a sunny spot and watch your celery grow.

4) BOK CHOY

You know how you cut the bottom of the bok choy off anyway? Well, if you pop that sucker into a bowl of warm water (the water should just cover the bottom) and leave it in a place with good light, it will soon reward your kindness with brand new leaves.

5) LETTUCE

After the celery and the bok choy, you know the drill! Just chop off the bottom of the organic lettuce, place it in a bowl with a little water and leave it in a sunny spot.

6) LEMONS

Lemon trees are awesome indoor plants and are easy as pie to grow. Just get an organic lemon and choose a couple of seeds. Don't let them dry out! Just pop them out of the lemon and plant about 1/2" (1.3 cm) below the surface of the soil. Water regularly and wait for your own little lemon tree to sprout.

7) BASIL

Look through your bunch of basil for a piece with a long stem and more than six leaves on it. Remove the top two and bottom two leaves and place the stem in a glass of water. Roots will appear within a week and before long, you can replant your basil and reap the rewards.

8) GINGER

Look for a ginger root with a small green nub. Plant it with the small green nub facing upwards and near the surface of the soil. Water, sunshine and love will see your ginger sprout in no time. Note: always use organic ginger as non-organic roots are treated with growth inhibitors. If you can't see any green nubs, place your ginger root in a warm, dark place and in a couple of days it will start to sprout on its own.

9) PINEAPPLES

This is a long-term commitment, but watching your pineapple grow and fruit will be a very rewarding experience. Start by breaking the top off your pineapple and trimming the bottom leaves to expose the base. Now stick 4 toothpicks around the base and suspend the pineapple top in a glass of water so that only the base is submerged. Once the small white roots appear, plant your pineapple and place in a warm, sunny spot.

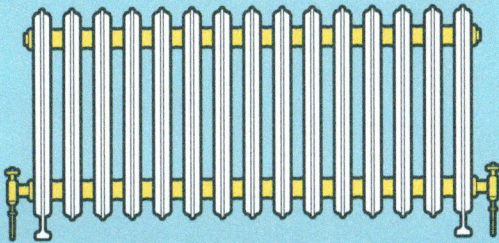

Save on heating bills by placing reflective material behind your radiators. That way you're heating your room rather than your walls. Open the valves on radiators to let out any air pockets and ensure that they are working optimally

LAUNDRY DETERGENTS

Make your very own suds with these easy recipes and avoid chemical cleaners which can irritate skin.

Use organic soap for the shaved bar soap component to be even greener. Washing soda and borax can be found in the laundry detergent isle at your local supermarket.

WHAT YOU NEED			
hot water	1/2 cup washing soda	1/4 cup borax	1/2 soap bar

INSTRUCTIONS

Fill a large pot with water and place on medium heat. Grate the soap into the water and stir until dissolved. Pour 2½ gallons (9.5 liters) of hot water into a bucket and add the soap solution, borax and washing soda. Stir until dissolved. Decant into empty bottles and use 1 cup in each wash. Mix before use. This solution will gel.

TIP

To make your veggies truly organic, avoid using pesticides. You can plant marigolds amongst your veggies to keep bugs at bay, use biodegradable soap in water to ward off worms and caterpillars and coffee grinds for unwanted pests.

STUBBORN STAIN DETERGENT

WHAT YOU NEED	
12 cups borax	8 cups grated bar soap
8 cups baking soda	8 cups washing soda

INSTRUCTIONS

Mix together. Use 1/8 cup of this washing powder for a large load. If you like your laundry to smell nice, add a couple of drops of essential oil to each load.

USES FOR USED COFFEE GROUNDS

Aside from making the world a happier place and fueling the start to your day, coffee has many other uses too. Don't dump your precious grounds when next you brew yourself a cup; there are so many environmentally-friendly things you can do with them!

FURNITURE STAIN

It's safe, environmentally friendly, organic and (unlike conventional stains) won't off-gas noxious fumes into your home for years to come. Make a natural, organic wood stain with your old coffee grounds. Brew yourself some strong coffee (let it steep for 4 hours). Apply with a rag and use a second dry rag to wipe off excess moisture. Leave overnight to dry.

Reapply two or three times depending on the color you want. This also works to hide scratches in dark furniture.

CELLULITE CURE

The caffeine in coffee grounds helps to break down cellulite. Rub the grounds onto your skin in a circular motion when you are in the shower. Grind of dry skin and get rid of cellulite for the double whammy win with a DIY sugar scrub: mix 1 cup course sugar with ½ cup coconut oil and add ½ cup coffee grounds. Rub onto the affected areas in a circular motion and rinse off for skin that's as smooth as a baby's bum.

FUNKY FRIDGE?

Just place a cup or mason jar of coffee grounds in your fridge to get rid of bad smells.

CLEAR OFF KITTIES

Sprinkle some coffee grounds in areas where you don't want cats to dig. Just a sprinkle will keep those pesky kitties at bay.

SHINY LOCKS

When you have washed and conditioned your hair, gently massage some coffee grounds through your locks for added shine and softness. Rinse and enjoy your new do.

MAKE TREASURE MAPS – NYAAAAARRRR!

Put some coffee grounds and a little water into a tray. Place sheets of paper in the solution and leave them for one minute. Gently remove (so as not to tear) and then let them dry. The coffee stains give your paper an antique patina. Now use the paper to create your own treasure map.

GROW BLUE HYDRANGEAS

Digging some coffee grounds into the soil increases its acidity. This makes it possible for hydrangeas to absorb more aluminum (which you can add to improve color) and turns the flowers blue.

> **TIP** Use a paste of baking soda and water to clean your oven rather than chemical cleaners.

> **TIP** Use glass jars and plastic take out containers as storage for lunches and leftovers.

TEACUP PLANTERS

Teacups make great planters for small herbs in the kitchen or small edible flowering plants like violas. I have used chipped teacups on their own very successfully as planters, but if you have a plant that requires good drainage, drill a hole in the center of the teacup with a ceramic drill bit before filling with potting soil. Of course the saucer makes a perfect drip tray to catch any excess water.

LOVE YOUR LOO

Turn your bathroom into an oasis with these organic recipes to replace just about everything in your medicine cabinet and makeup bag.

•••

Winter can really dry out your lips, or perhaps your perfect pucker just hasn't been the same since the great cooties outbreak of the 1990's. Most lip balms are packed with unnatural ingredients that can leave your lips feeling even dryer. Here are some really awesome recipes for making your very own lip balms. You can package these in decorative tins as gifts too.

BASHFUL BEESWAX BALM

WHAT YOU NEED	
5 tsp. jojoba oil (or coconut oil in a pinch)	3 tbsp. grated unbleached beeswax
6 drops essential oil (mint, lemon, lavender and peppermint are all great options)	
1 tsp. honey	

INSTRUCTIONS

In a double boiler* melt the beeswax and the oil together over low heat. Now chuck in the honey and essential oil and give it a good stir. Pour into tins or plastic containers and allow to cool for 20 minutes.

? Don't have a double boiler? Get a small pot filled with water and float a glass or metal bowl in the water.

Avoid products that are scented with rosewood. Over-havesting of the Brazilian rosewood tree has devastated populations in the Amazon.

SUPER SEXY SENSATIONAL LIP BALM

This recipe is especially good for lips that need a little extra attention. If you have chapped lips, this balm will get them smooth and kissable in two shakes of a lamb's tail.

WHAT YOU NEED	
I tbsp. avocado oil	2 tbsp. sweet almond oil
I tbsp. coconut oil	I tbsp. + I tsp. beeswax
2 tsp. essential oil (mint, lemon, lavender and peppermint are all great options)	
I tsp. vitamin E oil	

INSTRUCTIONS

Melt beeswax with avocado, almond and coconut oil in a double boiler over low heat. Remove from heat and add essential oil and vitamin E. Stir well and pour into lip balm tins. Leave to cool for 20 minutes.

TIP

Chemical hair dyes are really bad for you and for the environment. Prolonged use has been linked to cancers of the lymph system, blood cancers and bladder cancer. Instead, use natural henna hair dyes to cover your curls.

MASCARA

Making up is hard to do when your choices are mostly chemical. Now you can make your own mascara from natural ingredients. It moisturizes, it thickens and it darkens your lashes like it's nobody's business.

WHAT YOU NEED	
I tsp. coconut oil	I I/2 tsp. beeswax
4 tsp. of aloe vera gel	New or used mascara tube (sterilized)
I-2 capsules of activated charcoal (find this at your health food store)	

INSTRUCTIONS

Place the coconut oil, beeswax and aloe vera in a small pot. Warm over a very low heat until completely melted. Remove from heat and add the charcoal. Stir really well. When it's cool enough, pour it into a mascara tube.

?

Don't have a funnel? Pour mascara into a plastic bag and then cut a small hole in one corner and use the bag to get it into the mascara tube. Voila! Your very own easy peasy DIY homemade natural mascara.

EYE LINER

WHAT YOU NEED		
2 tsp. coconut oil	4 tsp. aloe vera gel	2 capsules of activated charcoal

INSTRUCTIONS

Mix well and apply with a small brush.

EYE SHADOW

WHAT YOU NEED	
arrowroot	spirulina for green
activated charcoal for black/gray	cocoa powder for brown
beet powder for pink	nutmeg for golden brown

INSTRUCTIONS

Start with ½ tsp. of arrowroot powder and slowly mix in as much of the color as you like. You can add more arrowroot if it's too dark.

Note: If you want a creamy eye shadow, mix 1/8 tsp. shea butter into your powder. This also helps to prevent the eye shadow from rubbing off.

FOUNDATION

WHAT YOU NEED	
arrowroot powder	finely ground organic cinnamon
organic cocoa	

INSTRUCTIONS

Start with an arrowroot base and then add tiny amounts of cinnamon and cocoa until you get as close as possible to your own complexion. Apply with a brush.

BATH BOMBS (FIZZIES)

WHAT YOU NEED		
8oz of cornstarch	4oz of baking soda	4oz of citric acid
3oz of cocoa or shea butter	3 tbsp. of almond oil	3 tbsp. of coconut oil
I tbsp. essential oil (optional)		

INSTRUCTIONS

In a plastic bowl, mix the cornstarch, baking soda and citric acid really well. Add the shea butter, almond and coconut oils and mix into a dough. Add your essential oils for scent (any kind you fancy) and add some natural food coloring if you want colored bath bombs. Now press into a small muffin tin, or an ice cube mold and leave to dry for 24 hours. Keep your bath bombs in a sealed container.

SHAMPOO

WHAT YOU NEED	
1 tbsp. baking soda	1 cup warm water

INSTRUCTIONS

Dissolve the baking soda in the warm water and pour it over your hair. Work it in and leave for 1 minute. Rinse well. It's so easy and so effective!

EGG AND OLIVE OIL CONDITIONER

WHAT YOU NEED	
2 eggs	3 tbsp. olive oil

INSTRUCTIONS

Mix ingredients in a bowl and work it into the hair from roots to tips. The olive oil will replenish dry hair and the protein in the egg will leave it shiny and give it bounce. Leave in for 5 minutes and then rinse with warm water.

HONEY & AVOCADO CONDITIONER

WHAT YOU NEED	
I avocado	I tsp. honey

INSTRUCTIONS

Mash the avocado in a bowl and mix well with the honey. Massage into your hair from roots to tips and leave for 5 minutes. Rinse with warm water.

If you suffer from oily hair or scalp, try ¼ cup of apple cider vinegar to remove excess oil. Rinse well.

The distinctive smell of moth balls comes from the release of toxic chemicals naphthalene and dichlorobenzene which are both bio-accumulative. Keep moths at bay the natural way with lavender sachets, cedar draws or rosemary sprigs.

BANANA FACE MASK

WHAT YOU NEED	
1/4 cup plain organic yogurt	3 tbsp. honey
1 medium banana	

INSTRUCTIONS

Mash up the banana and mix well with other ingredients. Gently apply to the face and leave for 15-20 minutes. Rinse well with warm water.

OATMEAL FACE MASK

WHAT YOU NEED	
1/2 cup hot water	1/3 cup oatmeal
2 tbsp. organic plain yogurt	1 egg white
1 tsp. honey	

INSTRUCTIONS

Mix the oatmeal into the hot water and leave for two minutes. Add the other ingredients and mix well. Apply to the skin and leave for 15-20 minutes. Rinse well with warm water.

APPLE CIDER VINEGAR TONER

WHAT YOU NEED	
2 tbsp. apple cider vinegar	2 cups water
4 tbsp. rose water (optional)	

INSTRUCTIONS

Mix ingredients together. Wash your face and then rinse with vinegar toner. Gently pat your face dry with a soft towel.

OLIVE OIL BODY LOTION

WHAT YOU NEED	
1/2 cup olive oil	1/4 cup coconut oil
1 tsp. vitamin E oil	1/4 cup beeswax
6 drops lavender essential oil	

INSTRUCTIONS

Combine ingredients in a glass jar and place in a small pot on the stove. Heat over a very low heat until all ingredients are in liquid form. Remove from heat, close the lid and shake the jar really well until all ingredients are mixed. Leave to cool. Apply to skin daily.

SUGAR SCRUB

↑

WHAT YOU NEED

1/2 cup course brown sugar	1/4 cup coconut oil

INSTRUCTIONS

Mix ingredients and rub onto the skin in a circular motion to remove dead skin cells. Add used coffee grounds to reduce cellulite.

NAIL STRENGTHENER

WHAT YOU NEED		
2 tsp. castor oil	1 tsp. wheat germ oil	2 tsp. sea salt

INSTRUCTIONS

Mix together and store in an airtight jar. Massage a drop of this strengthener into your nails every day. Wipe off excess with a cotton swab.

CUTICLE CREAM

WHAT YOU NEED		
0.5oz cocoa butter	1.5oz shea butter	1 tsp. glycerin
10 drops lemon essential oil	1/2 tsp. vitamin E oil	

INSTRUCTIONS

Place the shea and cocoa butter in a small pot and melt over a very low heat. When in a liquid state, remove from the heat and add remaining ingredients. Leave to cool overnight. Massage cuticle cream into the cuticles daily.

Commercial shoe polishes are crammed with unhealthy chemicals. Instead use a tablespoon of olive oil and a couple of drops of lemon juice. Rub into the leather, leave for a few minutes then buff with a soft, dry cloth.

LAVENDER HAND CREAM

WHAT YOU NEED		
1/3 cup almond oil	3 tbsp. coconut oil	3 tbsp. olive oil
25 drops lavender essential oil	3 tbsp. grated beeswax	

INSTRUCTIONS

Place almond, coconut and olive oil in a glass jar. Place it in a pot of water and warm over low heat until the oils have melted and combined. Remove the jar from the pot and add beeswax. Leave to cool for 10 minutes then add the lavender oil and mix well.

TOOTHPASTE

Does your mouth have a hankering for something fresh, natural and homemade? Well, we've got just the thing for you. If fluoride gives you the creeps or you just don't like the idea of chemicals in toothpaste, then go ahead and make your own! Ingredients like salt and baking soda provide stain-busting properties and act as mild abrasives to give tartar the boot. Peppermint, sage and lemon kill bacteria and add taste to your paste.

SUPER SIMPLE TOOTHPASTE

WHAT YOU NEED	
1 tsp. baking soda	1/2 tsp. sea salt (fine)
1 drop peppermint essential oil	A few drops of water

INSTRUCTIONS

If you only have course sea salt, grind it down in a mortar and pestle or in your coffee grinder. Mix all ingredients in a little bowl until you get a paste. Smear on your toothbrush and give it a go!

TIP Shell out less by saving water you boiled eggs in for your plants. It's enriched with calcium which they love.

YUMMY REMINERALIZING TOOTHPASTE FOR KIDS

WHAT YOU NEED	
3 tbsp. baking soda	1 tbsp. sea salt (fine)
1/2 tsp. finely ground dried sage	coconut oil, chilled to a soft paste
3 drops peppermint or spearmint essential oil	

INSTRUCTIONS

If you only have course sea salt, grind it in a mortar and pestle or a coffee grinder. Mix the dry ingredients and add the essential oils. Feel free to add more peppermint or spearmint if it needs a little zing. Now add one teaspoon of coconut oil at a time until you have a paste that your little champ can scoop up onto their toothbrush. Keep your natural homemade toothpaste in a cool place or the coconut oil will liquefy.

SUPER MINTY PARTY IN YOUR MOUTH TOOTHPASTE

WHAT YOU NEED		
6 tsp. baking soda	1/3 tsp. sea salt	15 drops peppermint
4 tsp. Bentonite clay powder (get this from a health food store)		

INSTRUCTIONS

Mix these ingredients together to form a paste and brush as usual. Now there's a party in your mouth!

DIY DEODORANT →

DINO TOOTHBRUSH RACK 60

YE OLDE FASHIONED TOOTH POWDER

WHAT YOU NEED		
2 tbsp. dried lemon rind	1/4 cup baking soda	2 tsp.sea salt

INSTRUCTIONS

Grind the ingredients in a food processor to create a fine powder. Now run your toothbrush under the tab and then dip the bristles into the powder and brush. Use this natural toothpaste to get that million-dollar smile!

DIY DEODORANT

Chemical antiperspirants may not be the best idea, but short of dousing yourself in patchouli, what choices do you have? You'll be pleased to know that you can make your very own deodorant in 5 minutes flat using items you probably already have in your kitchen cupboard.

WHAT YOU NEED	
2 tbsp. corn starch	2 tbsp. baking soda
2 tbsp. coconut oil	empty antiperspirant or plastic container

INSTRUCTIONS

Mix the ingredients together and spoon them into the container. Place them in the fridge until solid. Voila! Instant antiperspirant.

VAPORUB

Clear the stuffy noses, tight chests and coughs that a cold may bring the natural way with this organic vapor rub. This recipe makes about 12oz of comforting ointment that is just what the doctor ordered.

WHAT YOU NEED	
1/2 cup olive oil	1 cup coconut oil
35 drops eucalyptus essential oil	30 drops mint essential oil
15 drops rosemary essential oil	15 drops lavender essential oil
10 drops camphor essential oil	3/4 cup grated beeswax

INSTRUCTIONS

1) Melt beeswax, olive oil and coconut oil in a double boiler* over low heat.
2) Remove from heat and add essential oils.
3) Stir well and pour into a small container.
4) Leave to cool for 20 minutes before use.

? Don't have a double boiler? Get a small pot filled with water and float a glass or metal bowl in the water.

HOMEMADE COUGH DROPS

WHAT YOU NEED		
I cup elder flowers	I/2 cup horehound	I/2 cup hyssop
I/4 cup lemon balm	5 drops menthol	2 cups water
I I/2 cups honey	2-3 tbsp. olive oil	thermometer

INSTRUCTIONS

1) Place water, elder flowers, horehound, hyssop and lemon balm in a pot over medium heat and bring to boil, then simmer on low for 30 minutes. Strain off 1 cup of liquid. Place in a pot on the stove, add honey and heat over a medium heat until it reaches 300°F (149°C). This can take up to an hour. If your liquid starts to burn before it reaches 300F (149°C), add a tablespoon of butter.

2) Use the olive oil to grease a baking sheet.

3) Just as the liquid reaches 300°F (149°C), add menthol and stir. Pour the liquid out into the baking sheet and leave until it is still warm, but cool enough to handle. Pull off pieces of the hardened candy and roll into lozenges, then place back on the greased baking sheet to cool completely.

4) If you live in a humid climate, you can dust the lozenges with slippery elm bark before storing in an airtight container.

COUGH SYRUP

WHAT YOU NEED	
4 cups water	1/4 cup ginger root (grated)
1/4 cup marshmallow root	1 tbsp. cinnamon
1/4 cup chamomile flowers	1/4 cup lemon juice
3/4 cup raw honey	

INSTRUCTIONS

Place water, ginger, marshmallow root, cinnamon and chamomile flowers in a pot over low heat and simmer until the water is reduced by half. Strain to remove the herbs, and leave to cool for 20 minutes. Add lemon juice and honey.

Rent sports equipment for occasional outings rather than buying stuff that will clog up your garage or basement.

BITCH-BE-GONE

If your job's getting you down or you're just feeling a little snippy, then you can spray the blues away with this wonderful DIY soothing spray. Studies show that lavender has the ability to calm the nerves, lower blood pressure and soothe the jagged soul. Works on kids, pets and cranky coworkers too!

WHAT YOU NEED		
1/2 cup water	spray bottle	20 drops lavender essential oil

INSTRUCTIONS

Combine ingredients, spray, relax. Repeat. Spray on your pillow just before bed for restful sleep. Wanna get fancy? Add any of the following to give a little kick to your calm:

- ½ tsp. witch hazel
- 15 drops rosewood essential oil
- 12 drops chamomile essential oil
- 5 drops jasmine essential oil
- 10 drops orange essential oil

TIP Squish your trash! It takes up less space in your bin and in the landfill.

DINOSAUR TOOTHBRUSH RACK

Perfect for museum buffs, fans of the Mesozoic Era, paleontologists and kids, these super easy DIY toothbrush holders are functional fun. Simply drill a hole in the back of a large plastic dinosaur toy that is big enough to hold a toothbrush.

TIP

Ladies, ditch those tampons! The cotton industry uses a quarter of the world's pesticides and the tampons themselves are bleached. Instead, opt for a silicone cup which you insert in the same way you would a tampon. Just give it a rinse once or twice a day and you're good. Not only can you save a ton of money and prevent health problems associated with bleach, you also never have to worry about running out of tampons.

TIP

Every two minutes in the shower, you are using as much water as a person in Africa uses in an entire day. That includes cooking, cleaning, washing and drinking! Keep your showers short and sweet and consider the old brush and wash so you get your teeth clean while you shower. Showers of 5 minutes or less use about half as much water as baths. Better still, share your shower with a friend for good green karma.

If you are being bugged by flies, bees and wasps, sprinkle a couple of drops
of eucalyptus oil in areas where you want to sit and keep these insects away.
Citronella, mint and clove oils can also make flies buzz off.

WINE BOTTLE LAMPS AND CHANDELIERS

72

CHAPTER 4

THE BEDROOM

Turn your bedroom into an oasis of health and happiness where you can relax and restore with these jolly green DIY projects.

LAMP SHADES

There's no really good reason to buy a new lamp when the world is filled with already-made items you can convert into upcycled lamps for your bedroom. You can get a lamp fixture from your local hardware store for a couple of bucks; the rest is just imagination and moxie.... Here's some ideas to get your creative juices flowing.

COCKTAIL UMBRELLA LAMP

Our next set of upcycled shades use balls or balloons and white glue to create rounded lamp shapes. You can stick practically anything on a balloon to make a lamp, let the glue dry, pop the balloon and presto! I have always loved cocktail umbrellas and I am so glad someone found a way to utilize them for something more permanent than a mimosa.

WHAT YOU NEED	
white glue	cocktail umbrellas
balloon or blow up beach ball (gives a rounder shape)	

INSTRUCTIONS

1) Blow up the beach ball or balloon.
2) Open the umbrellas and break off the stems.
3) Use the white glue to attach them to each other around the ball or

COCKTAIL UMBRELLA LAMP ←

UPCYCLED LAMP SHADES 66

MASON JAR LAMPS

↑

WHAT YOU NEED

mason jar	goggles	gloves	drill
light socket with switch (get these from your hardware store)			

INSTRUCTIONS

1) Drill a hole through the lid of the Mason Jar, feed the light fixture cord through until the fixture is just below the lid.

2) Screw a light bulb into the fixture, then put the lid back on the jar. Attach a plug to the end of the cord and then there was light!

You can opt for a single jar, add additional fixtures for a string of lights or hang a bunch together for a Mason Jar Chandelier.

balloon. Try to minimize the amount of glue you get on the balloon. Leave a small hole through which to remove the balloon or ball

4) Leave to dry, pop balloon or deflate ball and remove.

5) Place the lampshade over the light fixture. You may need to secure it with string or ribbon.

UPCYCLING EXISTING LAMP SHADES

If your lampshades are dull, dusty or just old fashioned, you can give them a completely sassy new lease on life with a pair of tights.

WHAT YOU NEED		
tights	scissors	glue gun

INSTRUCTIONS

Patterned tights work best for these kinds of lampshades, but I have seen very effective ones made out of colored tights too. It really couldn't be easier; just pull the tights over the lampshade, then cut them above and below the lampshade, leaving a little seam which you can tuck under the rims and secure with a glue gun.

DOILIES LAMP SHADE

Doilies; I've never liked them… but when a friend recently gave me a bag of these little lacy layabouts, I was amazed at the intricate designs and the time and effort that must have gone into making them. The stitches were so fine and the thread so delicate I found myself reticent to toss them out. This funky little doilies lampshade upcycling project means you don't have to toss grandma's lacy bits.

WHAT YOU NEED	
I large bottle of white glue	beach ball
paintbrush	wire (I used an old coat hanger)
needle and thread	light bulb
light socket with switch (get these from your hardware store)	
ribbon	

INSTRUCTIONS

1) The first step is to inflate the beach ball. I used a small one on my first attempt, but there is no reason why you can't think big. I have seen these made with giant exercise balls too.
2) Once you have the ball inflated, lay the first doilie on the top.
3) Mix the white glue with a little water (I used a 20% water to 80% glue mix) and then paint the doilie with the glue mixture. The added weight made the ball roll over, so I stabilized it in a salad bowl. Don't worry

about the glue getting stuck to the bowl or the ball–it washes off easily!

4) Keep adding doilies around the top half of the ball. Ensure that the edges of the doilies overlap and stick together. Leave overnight to dry.

5) When the glue has dried completely, gently turn the ball over and repeat the process on the other side. Leave a gap over the valve so that you can deflate the ball. This gap should be big enough to fit the light bulb in. Leave to dry overnight.

6) Once your doilie lamp is dry, deflate the beach ball and remove. I trimmed the hole so that it was nice and round with a scissors. Cut a length of wire from your coat hanger and bend it into a ring.

7) Sew the wire ring around the hole in your doilie lampshade so that it provides added support.

8) Secure to the light fitting with ribbon.

Rugs at your front and back doors will help reduce the need to clean your floors.

WINE BOTTLE LAMPS AND CHANDELIERS

If you're anything like me, you always have a couple of wine bottles lying around and these are perfect for lamp shades. If you don't have a couple of empty wine bottles around, then this upcycling project is the perfect excuse to get to a wine store today!

WHAT YOU NEED			
wine bottles	glass cutter	gloves	goggles
light socket with switch (get these from your hardware store)			

INSTRUCTIONS

1) Don your gloves and goggles for protection (safety first!) Use the glass cutter to score a line around the base of the wine bottle. Put a thick elastic around the bottle if you need help getting a straight line. Once you have scored the bottle, alternate between putting it in very hot and very cold water until it cracks along the line and the bottom falls off.

2) Use some fine-grit sandpaper to smooth the cut line so that it is free of any chips and won't cut an unwary finger.

3) Now simply feed the cord from the light assembly through the neck of the bottle, attach a plug and screw in your light bulb. You can hang individual lamps from a hook, or group a bunch of bottle lamps together to make a chandelier.

4) Wine bottle lamp shades are a little trickier to make and I urge you to take every precaution to avoid injury when cutting the glass. Another thing to consider is the light that's created by different color wine bottles. I have found brown bottles give off a really warm and inviting glow and green is serene.

TREE BRANCHES LAMP SHADE

This is a great idea for a more rustic look if you want to bring organics back into your home and this lamp shade is perfect for the nesters.

WHAT YOU NEED	
white glue	balloon or beach ball
twigs	garden shears

INSTRUCTIONS

1) Snip the twigs off into 4-inch (10cm) lengths. Blow up your balloon or beach ball. Now glue the twigs to each other until they cover half of the ball. Try to get as little glue on the ball or balloon as possible.
2) Leave overnight to dry.
3) Flip it over and cover the other side with twigs, leaving an opening from which to remove the ball or balloon and to insert the light bulb.
4) Attach to the light fixture with string or ribbon.

TEACUP CANDLES

I love candles because they always cast you in the best light! They are warm and inviting and green too because you are saving electricity. Soy and beeswax candles are always preferable to the regular petroleum-based ones

This is a great way to use old candles and teacups. These cute cuppas make the perfect gift!

WHAT YOU NEED		
wooden skewer	string	teacup
old candles	double boiler	

INSTRUCTIONS

1) Break up the old candles and melt in a double boiler. If you don't have one, float a glass bowl in a pot of boiling water and melt the wax in that. I use an old camping pot so I don't have to clean it after each use.
2) While the wax melts, cut a length of string and tie it to the wooden skewer. It should be just long enough to touch the bottom of the teacup.
3) Pour the molten wax into the teacup and lay the skewer over the rim so the string hangs down into the middle of the cup.
4) Leave to cool.

FACING PAGE

SLIDE STAINED GLASS WINDOW LAMPSHADE

I vividly remember sitting on the carpet in my grandparent's home looking at grandpa's slides. He would collect them all through the year and fill a carousel with memories we would all enjoy sharing. We've since had all the old snaps transferred to digital, but I just couldn't bear to toss all those treasured collections.

If you have some family slides, don't throw them in the bin! You can use them to create fantastic lampshades which look a little like stained glass windows.

WHAT YOU NEED	
old cylindrical lampshade	3/8" (1 cm) jump rings
photo slides (you will need about 100-120 for a medium lamp shade)	
lamp base	1/8" (3.2 mm) hole punch

INSTRUCTIONS

1) Take the cover off the lampshade leaving only the frame.
2) Using the 1/8" (3.2 mm) hole-punch, punch a hole in all four sides of each slide, with the exception of the slides that will go along the bottom edge which should only be punched along three sides.
3) Assemble the lamp shade and the base so that you have a solid frame to work with. Attach the first row of slides to the top of

the frame with the jump rings and to each other on both sides. Continue on down the lampshade until you get the bottom. Turn the light on, and watch it glow – it makes great patterns on the walls!

You can also make a sheet of these slides connected with jump rings. Hang them over your windows as an awesome blind.

DIY HEADBOARD

Make your own headboard in just a few easy steps. This DIY is for a fabric-covered headboard, but you can also use old doors or wrought-iron fencing as vintage headboards.

WHAT YOU NEED		
plywood or osb sheet	saw	fabric
staple gun	screws	drill

INSTRUCTIONS

1) Simply cut the plywood or OSB sheet to the size (and shape) you want. Cover with fabric and secure at the back of the headboard with staples.
2) If you want a padded headboard, cut a piece of foam the same size as your headboard and glue onto your plywood or OSB sheet before adding the fabric.
3) Use the drill and screws to secure the headboard to your box spring.

CRUTCHES SHELVES

Look in the basement of most homes, and you will probably find an old pair of wooden crutches from an unfortunate childhood injury (there are two pairs of crutches in mine!) If you don't have a pair, you can pick some up from a charity shop for a couple of dollars.

WHAT YOU NEED		
crutches	saw	hinge
screwdriver	wooden planks	screws

INSTRUCTIONS

1) Turn the crutches upside down and remove the plastic caps from the bottom. Use the saw to remove the round bottom of the crutches so that you have rectangular ends.

2) Now join the crutches by screwing the hinge into bottom of both crutches where you sawed the round ends off.

3) Cut your wooden planks to size so that they fit on the two doweling struts of the hand support and the underarm support. This will mean that you have four planks which will act as shelves.

4) Position the crutches in an upside-down 'V' so that the hinge is at the top and the underarm supports are at the bottom. The smallest (and shortest) plank should be on the first doweling support under the hinge.

5) Place the plank on top of the doweling supports and screw it to the

crutch legs on the front and back. Repeat with all the planks until your crutch shelf is complete.

GREENING YOUR SEX LIFE

Sex is a great way to lose weight, reduce stress and lower your blood pressure. It can also be a great way to cut your carbon footprint which (inevitably) saves you some money. So here's how to slip into something a little more sustainable.

TURN YOUR LIGHTS DOWN LOW
Turn off the lights and turn up the atmosphere with candles. Unfortunately, most candles are made from paraffin wax (a petroleum product), so when you're burning candles, you're actually burning fossil fuels. What you really need is a beeswax or soy candle. Using candles means your electricity bill will be lower so turn off the TV, turn down the lights and, if you're feeling particularly athletic, turn down your thermostat too!

EAT YOURSELF FRISKY!
Combining my two favorite things is a match made in heaven. If you aren't always in the mood, you can eat yourself frisky with natural aphrodisiacs. Let's start with chocolate… chocolate contains phenylethylamine (PEA) which is a stimulant that boosts mood and reduces stress. Other frisky foods are pumpkin seeds, ginger, oysters and celery. There's some health store products that will help like ginseng, kelp, ginko biloba, and (lest we forget) horny goat weed.

ORGANIC PERSONAL PRODUCTS

Did you know that Americans spend $80 million a year on personal lubricants? Many of these contain some pretty nasty chemicals that are more suited to the auto industry. The ludicrously lucrative lube industry is unregulated and many products have been shown to be toxic. Opt for organic, non-toxic personal products that don't contain parabens or glycerin.

SEXY SKIVVIES

Go for organic cotton, sustainable bamboo, silk or soy or other sustainably-grown organic materials. If you must lycra, then opt for undies that are made from recycled plastics. The same goes for bed sheets, blankets and pillows… but why stop there? Get a green bed and base for a more natural, healthier home.

SHOWER SHARING IS PLANET CARING

Taking a long, hot shower solo is bad for the environment, but taking a long, hot shower with a friend is green living at its best. Taking a hot bath with a friend is equally good, especially if you're using organic soaps and hair-care products which you can follow up with an organic oil massage.

Does your office give you the blahs? You spend so much time there that you really need to make your office space a healthy and

The earth gets enough power to run for an entire year from just two minutes of sunshine. Home and business owners are increasingly turning to solar and installing PV panels. Consider this option as a long-term power solution.

THE OFFICE

serene place which reflects the wonder that is you. Green living in the office is easy and awesome and it saves money and gets you major points with the boss.

Start by substituting all your chemical cleaners for natural ones which is not only a huge money saver, it will help to improve the air quality too.

Recycle (always!) and suggest ways in which you can reduce the amount you print. Implement water and energy saving and make sure you turn off your lights and lower the thermostat when you leave the office. Floral friends are a must! Plants make the place look better, clean the air and elevate mood. Turn your cubicle into a jungle where everyone will want to hang out.

Go for vintage furniture. It's chic and fashionable and it means that you save money and reduce waste. An added bonus is that vintage furniture has already off-gassed all those noxious chemicals so you can breathe easy.

STANDING DESK

Do you sit for more than six hours a day? Your sedentary work environment is wheeling you and your office chair to an early grave. (Postulations that work is actually killing me? Confirmed!) Studies show that people who sit for more than six hours a day are likely to die younger than their more mobile counterparts. Luckily, an easy solution is at hand...the standing desk.

The standing desk has a small, but dedicated following. So fast is its popularity growing, that most office retail outlets now stock standing desks.

Guerrilla office workers have taken on a more 'MacGyver' approach to turning themselves into upstanding employees; using boxes, TV dinner trays and chairs to help raise their computers. Go on, give it a try. It does take some getting used to and you might want to phase it in.

Many companies are also opting for standing meeting areas. Here employees gather around a raised meeting table to exchange ideas and information in the same way you might stand around the kitchen at a party. This is thought not only to improve health, but also leads to a more fluid and interactive exchange of ideas.

IMPROVING INDOOR AIR QUALITY

Feeling tired, moody or like you're getting the flu? Poor indoor air quality in your office may actually be making you physically ill. One of the basic tenants of reducing energy costs is improved insulation. But this has resulted in buildings so airtight that indoor air quality is compromised. In many older buildings (especially those insulated after the energy crisis in the '70s) the indoor air quality can be as much as two to five times more polluted than outdoor air.

Poor indoor air quality is caused not only by a lack of adequate air circulation, but also by the release of volatile organic compounds (VOCs). VOCs can be released from PVC, building materials, finishes, paints, fire retardants etc. Chemical pollutants (like cleaning products) and biological pollutants (bacteria, mold spores, dust mites, pollen and viruses) are also detrimental to indoor air quality.

Known as sick building syndrome (SBS), illnesses that result from poor indoor air quality are difficult to diagnose. The main reason for this is that there are a large range of associated symptoms which affect people differently. Symptoms can include headaches, congestion, skin and eye irritation, coughing, difficulty breathing, asthma, edema, lethargy and chest pains. Symptoms are exacerbated when in the building, but may continue even when people have left. Some symptoms are temporary while others can lead to long-term, permanent conditions.

Sick building syndrome is not confined to older buildings and it is estimated that up to 30% of new buildings are also afflicted with poor indoor air quality. Get your building tested by a professional. If your building is in need of a breath of fresh air, there are ways to improve the situation. Although air filtration systems help, there is no substitute for good ventilation. Revamp your HVAC system and ensure that there is adequate outdoor ventilation. Remove VOC-producing building materials and opt for natural, environmentally-friendly alternatives.

If mold spores are detected, employ the services of a professional mold-removal company. Mold is insidious and can be embedded in walls, grow in ducting and entrench itself in your HVAC filters. The very act of cleaning it can release millions of spores which will only seed

When considering hardware upgrades, opt for laptops instead of desktops as they use 90% less energy.

more colonies. The spores themselves can cause many of the worst SBS symptoms.

Consider using pot plants to filter your indoor air. They have the added benefit of reducing stress. Plants are able to process VOCs and can filter up to 60% of airborne pollutants while adding aesthetic appeal to your building.

RANDOM ACTS OF KINDNESS FOR A HAPPY OFFICE

We've all been there; an office space that you hate, with colleagues you loathe which makes you more miserable than a zucchini on Meatless Monday. Making your office a happy place means changing the vibe and creating a positive atmosphere that benefits everyone. Small acts of kindness make the office a healthier, happier place to spend a third of your life.

VENDING MACHINE MAGIC

Tape an envelope to the vending machine with enough change to pay for the next person's snack. Make it a healthy one!

THE REXIES

I spray-painted a large plastic T-Rex gold and turned it into a trophy for the most awesome person in the office every month. I awarded it to the first person anonymously with a note listing all the nice things I had seen them do for other people in the office. I asked them to keep the trophy for a month and then pass it on to another employee with a list of all the reasons why they were awesome. There's nothing like public recognition to encourage your team to treat each other with consideration.

BRING A DOG TO WORK

Provided no one is allergic, allow a co-worker to bring their dog to work for a day. Petting animals has a soothing effect on people.

EMAIL APPRECIATION

Start every day on a positive note by writing an email to thank or praise someone you know. It can be a colleague, a client or a friend, but thank them for something they did or recognize a job well done.

FLOWER POWER

Bring flowers for someone who is having a hard time at work. Leave them on their desk with a note of encouragement.

POTTED PERFECTION

Pot plants help to elevate mood, clean the air and provide a wonderful atmosphere for your office mates. Get a couple of plants and place them around the office to brighten up the place a little.

COFFEE KLATCH

Going on a coffee run? Get someone else a cup too.

SHARING IS CARING

People feel great when they participate in random acts of kindness, so organize charity-orientated events at the office. Ask co-workers to bring in unwanted items and sell them online and donate profits to a charity of their choosing. Or ask them to bring in old clothing and call for a pick-up by a charity organization.

POST-IT PLEASANTRIES

Stick post-it notes on random pages of your office manuals and other books. People who have to consult the manual are probably having a tough day and could use a joke or an inspiring note.

NEAT TREATS

Bake or bring treats for co-workers and leave them in the communal kitchen.

CHOCOLATE CHEERINESS

Leave a chocolate on a co-worker's desk or leave a basket of candy in the office kitchen for everyone to share.

CUBICLE CREATIVITY

Encourage your co-workers to decorate their cubicles by offering a great prize to the best office space. Decorating cubicles will make your office a more interesting place to work.

POTLUCK LUNCH

Take turns making lunch for small office groups or organize a potluck where colleagues share their favorite dishes. This will mean healthier meals for office workers, less take-out waste produced and you will strengthen office ties.

PERSONALIZED MUGS

Mornings are hard, luckily there's coffee! You can make these fun DIY coffee mugs or tea cups for your favorite morning person. All you need is an old coffee mug or tea cup and a little creativity. Wow your neighbors, impress your friends and save the planet by upcycling coffee mugs rather than buying new ones.

WHAT YOU NEED
coffee mug, tea cup or other ceramic dishware
ceramic paint and paint brush, or permanent marker

INSTRUCTIONS

Wash the mug with soap and water and dry well. Use the paint brush to decorate it or use the permanent marker to create your masterpiece. Always work in a well-ventilated room. If you are using ceramic paint, leave your mug to dry for at least 24 hours.

If you are using a permanent marker, bake your mug in the oven for 30 minutes at 350°F. Leave to cool before using.

PICTURE FRAME BLACKBOARDS

These are fun anywhere in the office or in the canteen for areas where notices change regularly.

WHAT YOU NEED		
old picture frame	blackboard paint	newspaper

INSTRUCTIONS

1) Remove the glass from the frame, clean and dry thoroughly.
2) In a well-ventilated area, lay the glass out on the newspaper and spray it with blackboard paint as directed by the manufacturer. Leave to dry.
3) Put the glass back into the frame and hang your new blackboard in a suitable place in your office.

TIP Recycle everything! When you recycle a pile of newspapers a yard high (0.9 meters) you save a tree from the chop.

THE GARDEN

Green your garden by cutting out pesticides, reducing the environmental impact of your lawn and creating a healthy oasis for your friends, family and other wildlife.

WINDOW GARDEN: MOSS BALLS

For many people living in an urban environment, light is scarce. Moss balls are a brilliant Japanese solution to tiny, dark shoe-box apartments. If you live in a basement or a poorly-lit apartment where plants usually come to die, then the moss ball is the thing for you. With these, you can (quite literally) create a luxurious oxygen-producing hanging garden.

WHAT YOU NEED				
Plants – ferns, mondo grass, herbs and orchids all function well in moss balls, but you could use all manner of plants to make these furry little friends.				
moss	water	string	potting soil	akadama clay

INSTRUCTIONS

Shake most of the soil off your plant roots, then wrap them in a little moss. Now mix equal parts of potting soil and akadama* clay with enough

? Akadama clay is very expensive. You can buy it from a bonsai supply store. If you do not wish to spend too much money on clay, you can use red clay or clumping kitty litter. Make sure the clumping kitty litter is natural with no odor controls and no additives. Clumping kitty litter is made of bentonite, a naturally occurring clay product.

water to make a ball around the moss and roots. Place moss over the top of the clay and wrap with string to keep in place. Water your moss balls once a week by dunking them in water. Hang them in a window or from the ceiling where they will have access to light.

AQUAPONICS

Grow your own fresh, organic, veggies using your fish tank! Aquaponics is a closed-loop hydroponic growing method that doesn't need soil. Basically, you pump the water from your fish tank (rich in nutrients from fish poo) through your hydroponic growing tray. The plant roots are bathed in nutrient-rich, oxygenated water that helps plants to grow. Plants, in turn, clean and filter the water that goes back into your fish tank.

What this means is that you can use a fish tank to fuel a veggie garden – right in your own home – no pesticides, no soil, and a constant supply of healthy greens!

WHAT YOU NEED			
fish tank with fish		plastic tub for a grow bed	wooden planks
screws	6" piping	clay pellets	non-toxic adhesive

INSTRUCTIONS

1) Get your fish tank up and running and get some little fishy friends in there.

2) Use the planks and screws to create a wooden frame above the tank to hold the grow bed. I found this to be an easier solution as it allowed me unfettered access to the tank for cleaning and feeding.

3) Use the piping to divert water from the pump into the grow bed. Cut a small hole in the bottom of the grow bed and attach a pipe to allow the water to drain back into the tank. Ensure that you use non-toxic adhesives and pipes that don't leach noxious chemicals.

4) Fill the grow bed with the clay pellets and sprinkle organic seeds over the top. Get ready to enjoy your locally-grown, organic greens. If you don't get enough light indoors to grow veggies, hang a grow lamp above the grow beds.

RAISED GARDENS

If you have a nook in your garden that receives at least eight hours of sunlight, you can create a raised veggie garden bed. With a little tending, you will be amazed at how much you get out of your small little bed.

WHAT YOU NEED			
1" × 12" boards (x4)	4" × 4" posts (x4)	screws or nails	spade

INSTRUCTIONS

1) Arrange the four 1" × 12" boards so that the ends meet to form a square. Use the spade to mark the locations of the four corners of the box.

2) Move the boards to one side while you dig 1-foot deep holes for the 4" × 4" posts. Place a post in each of the holes and fill with soil.
3) Press the soil down firmly around each post to stabilize it.
4) Position the 1" × 12" boards into the square box shape and attach them to the posts with screws or nails.
5) Use the spade to turn the soil in the bottom of your raised garden, then fill your square with a growing medium of your choice.
6) Plant your veggies and enjoy organics with no carbon footprint!

DIY GREENHOUSE

Greenhouses can be made from just about anything. Some popular DIY options include greenhouses made from discarded windows or PVC piping and plastic. I use old clear plastic takeout containers as mini greenhouses when planting new seedlings into my garden in the spring to protect them from surprise late frosts.

Even if there aren't late frosts, the moisture and warmth their little dome provides certainly aids plant growth. Mason jars or any glass jars work well here too!

My favorite greenhouse (and one I have used for several years now) is an old wooden shelf I covered with plastic. Just buy sheets of plastic at your hardware store and staple them to the outside of the shelf. I left the front two sheets unsecured so I can pick them up out of the way when I want to tend to the plants.

GUERRILLA GARDENING: SEED BOMBS

This is the art of greening urban spaces and creating food sources that are local and organic. Guerrilla gardeners are the guys who create neighborhood vegetable gardens in abandoned lots or plant flowers in old cars; anything to make the city greener and more productive.

The most important weapon in the arsenal of the guerrilla gardener is the seed bomb. Seed bombs are ready-made planting factories just waiting for a friend to toss them in a bit of dirt. Here organic seeds are enclosed in a clay ball that can be dropped on any spare patch of ground. When the first rains fall, the clay ball dissolves and the seeds sprout.

Seed bombs can be kept in pockets, in cars and in bags so you can just lob them anywhere you find a dull ditch that needs a little love.

WHAT YOU NEED	
5 parts dry red clay or unscented clumping cat litter	
3 parts compost	organic seeds

INSTRUCTIONS

Mix the clay or cat litter with the compost and just enough water to make a playdough-like consistency that sticks together. Take a gumball-sized portion of dirt, stick a seed into the center and roll the clay around it into a ball. Leave to dry, then aim, fire and kabloom!

FACING PAGE

MOSS GRAFFITI

If you like the power of the painted word, but balk at inhaling noxious chemicals or being bust by the cops, then there are perfectly harmless ways for you to have your say in a pretty spectacular fashion. Green graffiti is the way modern, eco-friendly underground prophets are choosing to express themselves.

WHAT YOU NEED		
handful of moss	2 cups yogurt	2 cups water
l/2 tsp. sugar	blender	paint brush

INSTRUCTIONS

Find moss in damp areas in your garden or in a wood near you. Rinse the moss and place it in a blender. Add 2 cups of yogurt, 2 cups of water, ½ teaspoon of sugar and blend until smooth. Now just paint it onto any surface with a paintbrush. You can paint signs or messages on walls, or cover items in your home or garden with the moss paint. Keep it damp by spritzing it with water from a spray bottle every couple of days. Your green graffiti or moss art will start to grow in no time at all.

TIP Ditch those office vending machines and equip your kitchen with cutlery and crockery so you don't use disposable cups, plates and coffee stirrers.

LAWN ALTERNATIVES

Unless you're a sheep farmer, there's just no need for all that grass. If you're wasting water, money and a good deal of your precious Saturday mowing the lawn like a chump, just stop that right now. Sure lawns are really lovely and green, but they use an enormous amount of water, gasoline, fertilizer and your sweet time. The US alone uses 800 million gallons of gas a year to mow lawns and that accounts for a whopping 5% of greenhouse gas emissions.

Consider an alternative lawn, reducing the amount of lawn you have or doing something useful with all that space. Here are some alternatives to the traditional lawn that will have you thinking twice about your patch of green.

DOWN THE GARDEN PATH

If you simply must have a lawn, then at the very least reduce the amount of lawn you have. Create interesting features in your garden like paths and beds. Garden paths can be constructed from just about anything. Garden ponds also make for fun features that take up lawn real estate and they can be very eco-friendly if they are run with solar-powered pumps.

VEG OUT

An increasingly popular movement in urban farming is to get rid of your lawn altogether and replace it with a vegetable garden. A word of caution here; if this is in your front yard, there may be local ordinances against veggie gardens and the city can ask you to remove yours if the neighbors complain. Check with your local municipality bylaws before you start ripping up your front lawn.

Vegetable gardens take surprisingly little work and produce bumper crops. Avoid artificial fertilizers and pesticides so that you have a ready supply of organic vegetables and fruits. Your veggie garden can look amazing if you take the time to landscape it a bit and add decorative flowers like marigolds to make it look nice and to keep bugs at bay. You can butter up the neighbors by offering a couple of free fruits and veggies when your cornucopia overflows.

COVER UP

Switch to a perennial ground cover. Ground covers use less water, require less maintenance and don't need to be mowed (yippee!) A really popular choice is microclover which spreads fast, looks great and flowers too. Opt for other hardy perennials such as dwarf dogwood, alyssum, tapien (verbena), sweet woodruff, cotoneaster, and bishop's weed. You can also plant herbs like juniper, thyme, chamomile, and oregano which make for luscious, fragrant carpets.

COMPOSTING

Composting is really an outside activity unless you want to practice vermiculture. Get some vermiculture worms from your local nursery or buy vermiculture kits online. This is usually a plastic bin filled with soil and worms. The runoff is collected underneath the bin and acts as a super strong fertilizer. In fact this fertilizer is so strong that you must dilute it before use.

Put a vermiculture box in your classroom. The kids get to learn about worms and they use the fertilizer on the school's veggie garden. They also really enjoy feeding the worms with their biodegradable lunch leftovers.

PALLET COMPOSTING BOX

This is a great way to create a small composting box at the bottom of your garden. Use wooden pallets to keep costs at a minimum.

WHAT YOU NEED		
5 wooden pallets	2 hinges	1 latch
screws (or nails)	screwdriver (or hammer)	

INSTRUCTIONS

Use the screws or nails to hammer four of the pallets together to create a box. Attach the 'lid' with the two hinges. Attach the latch onto the front so you can secure the compost box against raccoons, squirrels, rats and other pests.

Fill your bin with lawn cuttings and biodegradables from your home. If you heard that peeing in your compost heap is a good idea, you would be right. Your pee adds valuable nitrates to the compost heap. Use a spade to turn the compost about once a month. Keep the compost heap moist in dry weather.

NATURAL PESTICIDES

For soft bodied insects like worms and grubs, soapy water really does the trick. Be sure to use natural, biodegradable soap which contains no chemicals.

FUNGAL DISEASES

Two tablespoons of baking soda in a liter of water will help with fungus. Pour it over affected plants or use a spray bottle to spritz leaves. Do this every three days until the fungus disappears.

For fungus gnats, symphylids, centipedes, root lice, aphids and plant lice, use a tobacco tea. Steep tobacco in warm water until it is the color of tea. Then spray on leaves or pour into the soil to get rid of pesky pests.

Got ants? Mix 10 drops of a citrus essential oil with one teaspoon cayenne pepper and 1 cup of warm water. Place in a spray bottle and spray areas ants frequent.

Flies, bees and wasps hate eucalyptus oil. Sprinkle a couple of drops around to keep these insects away.

Chrysanthemums contain a powerful chemical component called pyrethrum which enters the nervous system of insects rendering them immobile. Boil 100 grams of dried Chrysanthemum flowers in 1 liter (about 2 pints) of water for twenty minutes. Strain, cool and place in a spray bottle and use as a general-purpose insecticide.

Another general-purpose pesticide can be made by grinding two handfuls of dry chilies into a fine powder and mixing with 1 cup of Diatomaceous earth. Add this mixture to 2 liters (about 4 pints) of water and leave to soak overnight. Shake and then spray or pour over affected areas.

DINO PLANTER

↑

WHAT YOU NEED		
toy dinosaur	Xacto knife	cactus and soil
VOC-free paint	paint brush	

INSTRUCTIONS

1) Carefully cut a hole in the back of the plastic dinosaur toy.
2) Paint with a VOC-free paint and leave to dry.
3) Fill the toy with sandy soil and plant your cactus or succulent.

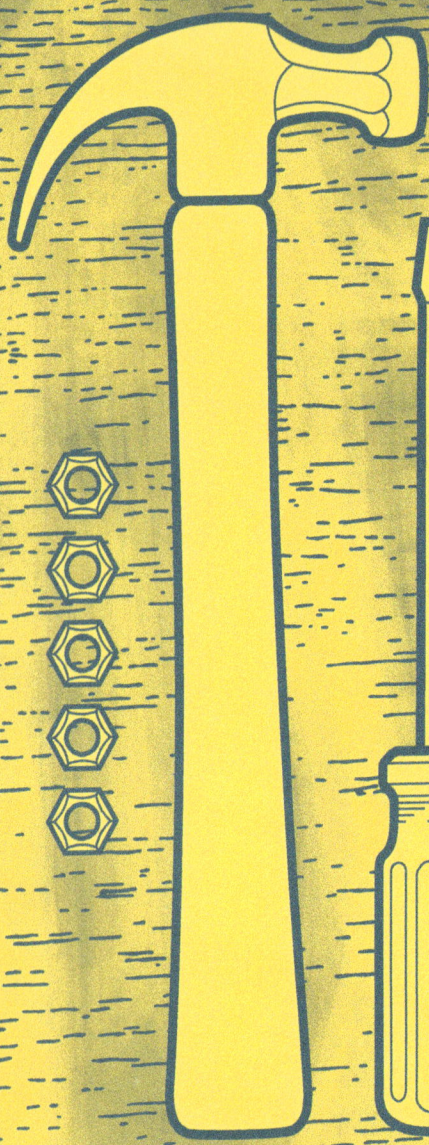

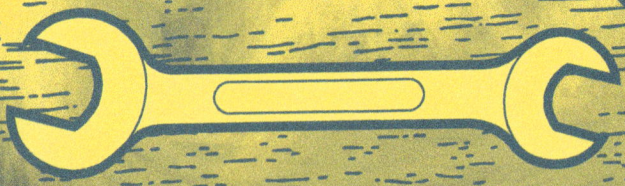

CHAPTER 7

HOUSEHOLD MAINTENANCE

Home maintenance can be time-consuming, costly and chemical, but doing a good job of keeping your castle can save you money and reduce your home's carbon footprint.

WINTERIZING

NATURAL DEICERS

Salt does do a great job of melting ice and snow through the winter but its bad news for your pets, the environment and your garden. Pets get salt on their paws which causes cracking, salt corrodes metal, damages concrete and wreaks havoc on your garden and lawn. With spring melt, all the accumulated salt ends up in your waterways where the local wildlife may not survive the seasoning. Here are some green living alternatives to melt your winter ice.

ORGANIC SALT-FREE DEICER

It's a little pricier than salt, but these products will help to keep your walkways and driveways ice-free.

Close your damper when you're not using the fireplace. Up to 8% of your home's heat can escape through open dampers which costs you $100 a year.

KITTY LITTER

Ok, this doesn't actually melt the ice, but it does provide traction for a more non-slip surface and the darker color causes the snow to melt faster.

UREA

This is a natural deicer and while it won't harm your pets, corrode your metal or pit your concrete, it can be really bad news for your plants so avoid using it near the garden.

ALFALFA MEAL

This is a super effective natural green ice melting miracle! It's 100% natural and is usually used as a fertilizer. It's grainy so it will provide traction and is extremely effective when used in moderation.

SUGAR BEET JUICE

The juice from sugar beets lowers the melting point of ice and snow which helps to clear your driveway. It's even been used to melt ice and snow on municipal roads in some areas. It's safe for animals, people, metals, concrete and plants.

SAND, ASH FROM THE FIREPLACE OR COFFEE GROUNDS

Sprinkle these over your icy surfaces to provide traction and the darker colors will absorb more heat and help to melt snow and ice.

Don't underestimate the importance of shoveling. A good shovel will clear your drive while giving you a wicked workout and it's the most natural, environmentally friendly way to get rid of your icy bits this winter.

WINTERIZING YOUR HOUSE

In the immortal words of Ned Stark; winter is coming. And when it does, not being prepared can be costly. Burst pipes, roof leaks and other cold weather woes can make the winter more miserable than it needs to be. Here are ways in which you can prepare your home for winter and seal it up tight so your precious warm air doesn't escape. You'll be saving money and the planet too!

FANDOM

Reverse the direction of your ceiling fans to help evenly distribute heat in your home.

DIY ENERGY AUDIT

Know where you are losing energy and get the most bang for your winterizing buck. Save even more by doing an energy audit yourself.

LEAK YOUR LIZARDS

Drain all outdoor hoses like the garden hose, the AC hose etc. If you have exposed pipes, wrap them in insulation to prevent bursting.

PROGRAMMABLE THERMOSTATS

Don't have one? Get thee to the hardware store stat! Using a programmable or set-back thermostat will lower the indoor temperature while you are at work or when you are sleeping so you can save 20-75% of your operating costs.

DEAL WITH DEAD BRANCHES

Cut dead or dying limbs from trees around your home or the weight of winter snow may send them crashing down on you.

FIX YOUR FURNACE

Get your vacuum out and clean your furnace and filters and suck up any dust around the coil. Change your filters regularly according to the manufacturer's instructions to maintain good air quality and improve efficiency. Check the outside flue to ensure that no vegetation or nesting birds are causing obstructions. Walk around your home and ensure that all the vents are open and clear.

Check your ducts for leaks and fix them with metal-backed tape (Note: ironically, this may be the only thing in the world for which duct tape is not the answer.) You can lose up to 60% of your heat when you have leaky ducts.

Take the cover off the air handler and check your blower belt. Replace if cracked or frayed. A few drops of oil on the moving parts won't hurt while you're at it!

GET AN ERV

Energy Recovery Ventilation (ERV) systems utilize heat from the furnace exhaust system to heat outdoor air before it comes into your home. This means you save 70% to 80% of the heat from the exhausted interior air while keeping indoor humidity at a comfortable 40% to 50%.

Now would also be a great time to check your smoke detectors and fire extinguishers. Nothing bums you out and adds to your carbon footprint like your house burning down. So bring it on, winter, you've got this.

CAULK YOUR HOME

According to the Earthworks Group, the average home has cracks that can add up to a 9 square foot hole in the wall. Caulk up cracks, holes and gaps, paying particular attention to plumbing, windows and other openings.

SEAL THE DEAL

Check rubber seals around doors to ensure that cold air isn't coming in. Windows: Double-paned are best, but if you need a cheaper fix, cover windows with bubble wrap or plastic window wrap which you can get from your local hardware store.

Over 60 million plastic bottles are disposed of in the US every day. Say no to bottled water and yes to savings by installing a water purification system in your kitchen. Buy reusable water bottles to transport your fresh water to work or school.

SUMMERIZING YOUR HOME

If spring is in the air, it is time to get your home ready for the summer heat.

AC TUNE-UP

- ACs running in the shade are up to 10% more efficient, so place yours in a shady place or create shade around it.
- Ensure it is not overgrown with vegetation.
- Change your filters and check ducts for leaks. Get washable filters to reduce costs and waste.
- Check indoor vents are clean and unobstructed.
- Vacuum the coil and any other dust from the unit.

CHECK YOUR HOSES FOR LEAKS

A dripping tap or hose can really add to your water bill, so check yours didn't crack or fray over the winter. Get a garden hose repair kit from the hardware store before you buy a new hose.

GET A PROGRAMMABLE THERMOSTAT

This will reduce your AC use during times when you are not home or at night. Check your window screens and replace any that are damaged or that you removed over the winter.

CEILING FANS

Reverse the winter rotation settings so that your fan can effectively circulate cooler AC air.

RECYCLING

Recycling is a great way to reduce habitat destruction and reuse valuable resources. While most cities have recycling schemes in place, here are a few tips on how to recycle more responsibly.

CHEMICALS AND PAINTS

Everything from paint stripper to fire-lighting fuel has noxious chemicals in it. When you need to get rid of old oil, gas, camping fuel, paint stripper, paint, brake fluid, antifreeze and any other chemical substance, ask your local municipality where you can do so responsibly. There is usually a drop-off center that will handle these for you. Don't toss them in the garbage as they end up in the landfill.

ELECTRONICS

Sell your used electronics to companies that refurbish them or distribute them to developing countries. You can also sell them to a salvage yard which will extract precious metals and take care of dangerous substances like mercury.

TIP

Riding your bike to work not only keeps you slim and healthy, every four-mile trip (about 6.4 kms) by bike prevents about 15 pounds (about 6.8 kgs) of air pollution.

APPLIANCES

These contain noxious gases, mercury and oil which can really pollute the environment. Call your local municipality to find out how to recycle them responsibly.

FURNITURE

Donate this to charity or consider a revamp. Often a fresh coat of paint and new upholstery makes all the difference.

CLOTHING

Clothing swaps are fun! You save money on new clothing and save the environment too. Get together with friends, family members or colleagues to exchange new or gently used items. Donate the rest to a charity of your choice.

RECYCLE EVERYTHING!

Need something? Consider buying it second hand. Vintage items are usually cheaper, help save valuable natural resources and have already off-gassed all their toxins which makes your indoor air quality so much better.

TIP

While only about 2.5% of the world's agricultural land is utilized for cotton farming, they use a quarter of the world's pesticides. Opt for organically farmed cotton whenever possible.

SAVING WATER

GO LOW WITH THE FLOW

- Low-flow showers and toilets help reduce consumption. If you don't have the money to install these, toss a plastic bottle of water in your cistern to reduce flush volume.
- Check washers to prevent leaks. Replace any that are cracked or frayed.
- Dishwashers use less water than hand washing, but ensure that the dishwasher is always full. Opt for an Energy Star approved model to save on energy too.
- Showers use less water than baths if you keep them under five minutes.
- Downspout extensions will redirect rainwater to your garden beds and lawn.
- Rain barrels make an excellent storage facility for rain water which you can use in the garden.
- Lawn alternatives like perennial ground covers reduce water consumption.
- Plant indigenous plants which are more likely to survive without additional watering.
- Spreading mulch under plants reduces the need to water and weed.
- Gray-water recycling directs water from showers etc. into your garden. Get even greener by redirecting gray water through a natural wetland which you can create in your yard.

SAVING ELECTRICITY

VAMPIRE LOADS

Did you know your appliances use power even when turned off? In fact, 5% to 10% of the energy used in your home is syphoned off for standby power. Unplug appliances or use 'smart' power bars with built-in timers to turn your appliances off when you're not home.

ENERGY STAR

Use Energy Star rated appliances as they have reduced energy requirements.

TURN IT DOWN!

Save 10% on your energy bills by reducing your thermostat by 20°F in the winter.

COLD WASH

Switch your washing cycle to cold to use 50% less energy on laundry day.

AIR DRY LAUNDRY

Don't use the dryer through the summer months when you can dry clothing outside.

ENERGY-EFFICIENT LIGHT BULBS

96% of energy from incandescent bulbs goes to producing heat rather than light. With compact fluorescents, you get four times more light per energy unit and they last 10 times longer.

DIY CLEANING PRODUCTS

Adverse to the utilization of elbow grease myself, I am partial to cleaning products that suggest their powerful chemical compositions will reduce the need for waxing on and waxing off. I'm quite happy to never be a ninja if it means I can simply spray something on the dirt and then get back under the duvet. And although it's true that commercial cleaning products contain enough chemical clout to vaporize small bacterial colonies, their astringent chemical compounds are harmful to you and your family and reduce the quality of your indoor air.

KITCHEN AND BATHROOM

Dust surfaces with baking soda and wipe down with a sponge. For stubborn stains and dirt, add a couple of drops of lemon juice or white vinegar. White vinegar and baking soda are excellent disinfectants.

ALL-PURPOSE CLEANER

WHAT YOU NEED	
l/2 cup white vinegar	l/4 cup baking soda
2 liters of water	

INSTRUCTIONS

Mix in a spray bottle and tackle household grime.

CLOGGED DRAINS

Pour a 1/4 cup of baking soda down your dirty drain followed by hot water to clear. Pour 1/4 cup of baking soda down your drains periodically to ensure that they stay clean.

OVEN

Make a paste with baking soda and water and smear it on. Leave overnight and wipe clean in the morning.

ODORS

Sprinkle baking soda over the offending area and leave for a couple of hours. Sweep or vacuum up.

WINDOWS

2 Tbsp. of white vinegar in a gallon of water (about 4 liters) is all you need. Spray onto the surfaces with a spray bottle and wipe down with newspaper for a smudge-free clean.

FLOORS

Up the vinegar content (about 1/4 cup of white vinegar to a 1/4 gallon of water) in your spray bottle. Spray on tile, linoleum, wood and parquet floors and mop as usual.

CARPET SPILLS

Sprinkle with salt to soak up and disinfect. If the stain is still visible, douse with club soda.

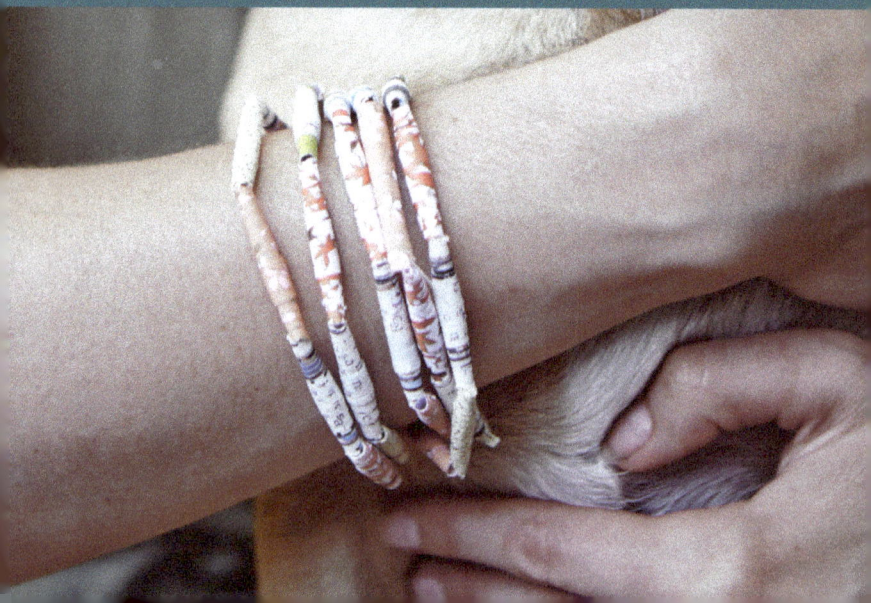

THE KIDS

Teach your kid some mad skills, have fun and make cool toys from used materials. These awesome upcycled and recycled toys are an easy and fun way to introduce basic electronics, photography, woodwork and science techniques.

SHOPPING BAG RAINCOAT

Kids grow so fast that it may be costing you a fortune to keep them dry. You can have a lot of fun making raincoats from old shopping bags instead of getting new ones.

WHAT YOU NEED	
plastic shopping bags	scissors
iron	parchment paper

INSTRUCTIONS

1) Cut the handles and the bottoms off the shopping bags so that you have a tube of plastic. Turn inside out so that the ink from the shopping bags doesn't get onto the iron. Set the iron to low heat (Rayon or Polyester setting) and let it warm up. In the interim, arrange your plastic bags on top of each other (that makes 4 layers) and so that they overlap adjoining bags. Place the bags between two sheets of parchment paper.

2) Slowly run the iron over the top of the parchment paper. You should be able to fuse the layers into one thick layer with about 15-20 second of ironing. Rub the plastic between your fingers to ensure that it has properly fused.

3) Continue to fuse the plastic bags together until you have one big sheet of plastic fabric. Now you can cut out a raincoat pattern and sew it together or make a rain poncho by cutting a hole in the middle.

4) You can also use this plastic fabric to line the underside of a blanket to keep it dry during picnics, as a tarp or as a waterproof cover for your backpack.

SUITCASE AMP

Here's a whole new way to get those sweet, sweet vintage suitcases you've had lying around to rock your world… and your neighbor's world too. This DIY amp is the instrument of champions.

WHAT YOU NEED		
old vintage suitcase	second hand amp	jigsaw
decorative edging (get this at the haberdashery)		screws
drill	superglue	electrical tape

INSTRUCTIONS

1) Disassemble the amp and separate the driver (speaker) from the control panel. You can do this by loosening the bolts that attach it to the frame of the amp. If you need to cut any wires, be sure to mark them first so you will know how to reattach them.

2) Find a position for the speaker and controls that suits your case. Trace around both of these and set them aside. Drill a hole along the traced line and use the jigsaw to cut out a hole for your speaker and another one for your control panel. Fasten the control panel to the wooden panel that the speaker is mounted to with some

screws. Fit it into the hole you cut into the suitcase and fasten together by screwing through the suitcase and into the wooden panel.

3) Re-attach any wires you cut before and secure with electrical tape. Use the drill to drill a hole in the side of the suitcase for the power cord. This is more of a notch than a hole as it should be situated where the top and the bottom of the suitcase meet along the side of the case.

4) Use the superglue and decorative edging to finish off the areas around the cuts you made in the suitcase.

TOYS FROM CARDBOARD BOXES

Cardboard boxes are the most versatile items in your recycling bin. With the big ones that appliances come in, you can cut out windows on the side to turn them into puppet theaters, shops and banks for the imaginative entrepreneur.

Smaller moving boxes can be placed on their sides, cut the top side open and turn it into an airplane, a race car, a rocket, a tardis or a train.

If you've recently moved, you can put a number of boxes together to form forts, castles and other grandiose dwellings. Turn smaller cardboard boxes into treasure chests or post boxes that require letters to Santa or the tooth fairy. Smaller boxes also make great stoves for the modern chef with the open end acting as the oven door.

Whether you are constructing planes, trains or automobiles (and boats!) you and your children can enjoy hours of fun creating and then playing with toys made from cardboard boxes.

TIP

Leave your lawn cuttings on the lawn. They will help to prevent evaporation so your lawn will need less water. Rotting grass cuttings will create a rich compost that returns nutrients to the soil. Make sure that the grass is dry when you mow so that the cuttings don't clump.

SKATEBOARD SWING

Turn old skateboards into swings in just two easy steps! They are comfortable and functional too.

WHAT YOU NEED		
skateboard	drill	rope

INSTRUCTIONS

Remove the wheels from the skateboard and drill two holes at both ends. Hang in a tree with the rope to make a swing. A cautionary tale: Always test the sturdiness of the branch before jumping on the swing.

DINOSAUR COAT RACK

Plastic dinosaurs can wreak havoc on unsuspecting villages, so you can keep your Lego men and women safe by turning old dinos into a new coat rack.

WHAT YOU NEED		
hacksaw	dinosaurs	plaster of paris
plank	screws	

INSTRUCTIONS

Use the hacksaw to cut the dinosaurs in half. Fill them with plaster of Paris and then leave them to set (balance them in a muffin tin or egg carton). Use the front ends or the back ends or both!

When set, space them evenly on the plank and screw them in place from the back of the plank. It looks nice if you sand the plank and use paint or clear vanish as a finish.

LED THROWIES

Add a splash of color to your home or neighborhood with these easy to make LED throwies for about a dollar each.

WHAT YOU NEED	
LED (any color)	electrical tape
CR2032 3V lithium batteries (watch battery)	
1/2" diameter x 1/8" thick NdFeB disc magnet (these are super strong magnets so keep them away from your credit cards!)	

DINOSAUR COATRACK

INSTRUCTIONS

1) Slip the battery between the LED wire leads so that the longer LED lead (the anode) is over the positive terminal (+) of the battery and the shorter LED lead (the cathode) is on the negative terminal (-) of the battery. The LED should light up, if it doesn't just flip the battery over and try again.

2) Wrap the tape around the battery and LED once, then place the magnet on the positive terminal and wrap the tape around again. Take aim and throw!

3) Throwies will stick to any ferromagnetic metal surface and they will glow for days or weeks. Please make sure that you throw them where you can retrieve them.

DOLL'S HOUSE

Got an old chest of drawers you don't need any more? Take the front of the drawers off and it instantly becomes a lovely dolls house. You can leave the last drawer or two for storage while you and your child decorate the interior of the house with furniture. Use gift wrap as fancy wall paper.

TIP Good news! If you use an energy and water-efficient model and only do a wash when its full, using a dishwasher is actually more environmentally friendly than hand-washing your dishes.

DIY LAVA LAMP

This is super simple and it's really effective.

WHAT YOU NEED			
vegetable oil	food coloring	water	alka seltzer

INSTRUCTIONS

Fill a plastic soda bottle ¾ full of vegetable oil. Mix food coloring with water and fill up the bottle with colored water (make it as dark as you can). Break the alka seltzer tablet into eight pieces. Drop in one at a time and close the lid of the bottle.

BIKE LIGHT FROM DEODORANT CAN

Bike lights are an essential component to safe biking, but you don't have to spend a bunch of money on them. Here's a great weekend project to do with your kids which teaches them about safety, basic electronics and solar energy.

WHAT YOU NEED	
empty deodorant stick	dollar store solar light
drill	glue gun

INSTRUCTIONS

1) Remove inside of the deodorant stick and pull out the screw mechanism.

2) Take the solar light apart so that you can remove the solar cell which should be wired to a circuit board and a battery pack. You will also need to locate the light sensor which is a little cadmium cell located near the solar panel. The cadmium cell acts as a switch which turns the light on when it gets dark.

3) Drill a hole in the broad side of the deodorant canister where the wires from the solar cell can go through. Glue the solar cell and cadmium cell to the top, run the wires through the hole you drilled and connect them to the circuit board and battery pack which go inside the body of the deodorant canister. Position the LEDs at the top and glue in place. Put the lid back on and attach it to your bike.

SNOWBALL GLOVES

WHAT YOU NEED			
gloves	plastic ball	scissors	glue gun

INSTRUCTIONS

Snowball fights are always fun, but if you don't like getting your gloves wet, just cut a plastic ball in half and use a glue gun to attach one half to each glove for the perfect snowball making machine.

DIY PVC PIPE PERISCOPE

WHAT YOU NEED	
PVC pipe cut into two 12" sections. One section should be slightly wider so that the other section can slide up into it	
two PVC elbow joints that are the same diameters as the two pipes	
two round mirrors	putty

INSTRUCTIONS

Use the putty to stick the two mirrors into the bends of the elbow joints at a 45° angle. Twist the elbows into the pipes and slide the narrow pipe into the wider pipe and you are done!

Buy earring, necklace, ring and bracelet findings at your local bead shop and get your kids to make jewelry out of old toys, stationary and other things around the house. For example, you can make earrings from Barbie shoes or Lego blocks.

PAPER BEAD NECKLACES

These are easy and fun to make, especially from gift wrap that you collect from special occasions. You can collect gift wrap from a wedding and craft a necklace for the bride or get your kids to make grandma a bracelet from last year's Christmas gift wrap.

WHAT YOU NEED		
wooden skewers	gift wrap	scissors
white glue	clear nail polish	

INSTRUCTIONS

1) Cut the gift wrap into small, long triangles. Experiment with the width of the base and the length of the triangles to find the right size for your beads. Then use that triangle as a template to cut the others.
2) Hold the skewer in one hand and place the wide side of the triangle on the skewer. The paper should be right side up.
3) Now wrap the paper around the skewer. When you get near the end, place a very small bead of white paper glue on the tip of the triangle and paste it down.
4) Paint the bead with clear nail polish. Leave to dry.

? You should have a number of skewers so you can continue to work while the beads dry. You can also paint your beads or decorate them with glitter for a little bling.

HOBBY HORSE

You don't have to be good at sewing to make this hobby horse. All you need is a stuffed sock, some felt for the ears and eyes and wool for the mane.

WHAT YOU NEED		
sock	stuffing	felt
ribbon or wool	broom stick	glue gun

INSTRUCTIONS

Fill the sock with stuffing. Cut eyes, nostrils and ears from felt and glue onto the horse's head. Push the broom stick up into the sock and add additional stuffing if necessary. Pleat the bottom of the sock and glue firmly to the broomstick all the way around. Glue wool or ribbon on for the mane.

TIP
When buying souvenirs, opt for those made by local families rather than commercial mass-produced items.

TIP
Avoid buying cut flowers as these are grown using pesticides, fertilizers and plenty of water, not to mention the carbon footprint of transportation and delivery. Instead opt for plants and locally grown, organic flowers.

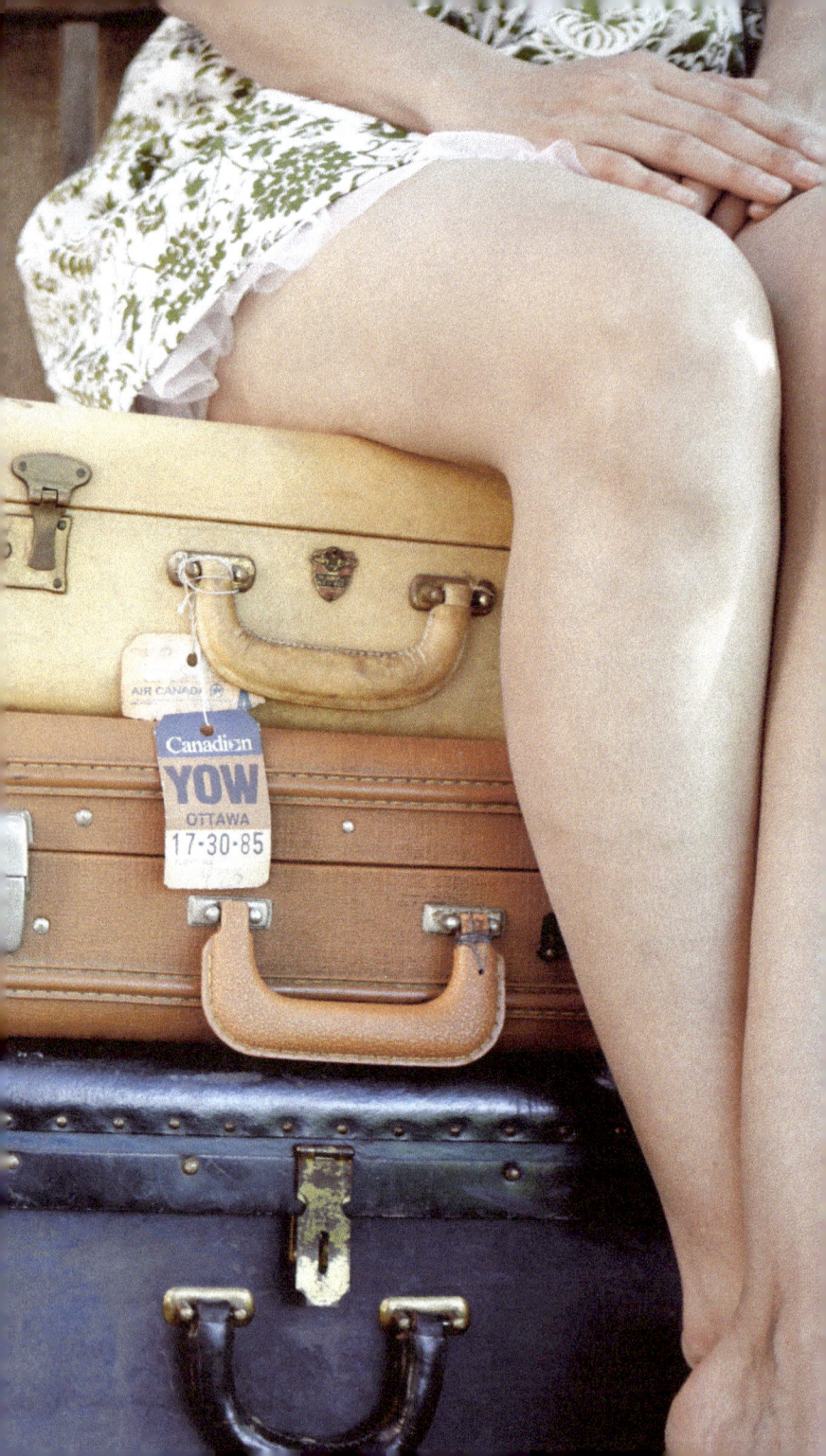

TRAVEL

Your leisure time or work travel doesn't have to be bad for the environment. Now you can have your holiday and enjoy it too with all these ways to reduce your carbon footprint en-route.

TRAIN GANG

Rediscover the glamor of train travel as this is a much greener way to get there. You can even treat yourself to that first class ticket – it's still cheaper than a flight. While it will take you longer to get there, you can relax, work, sleep or catch up on movies while you rediscover the joy of the journey.

ROAD TRIPPING

If you must go by road, turn your solo run into a road trip with friends or family members. Carpooling is a far more efficient way to travel than by air.

FLY SMART

Opt for a direct flight and fly during the day as take offs and landings use the most fuel and planes use more fuel at night.

TAKE NOTHING BUT FACEBOOK PICTURES, LEAVE NOTHING BUT LOVE:

- Avoid take-out packaging waste by making your own meals.

- Shop at local markets to support local artisans and families and reduce the carbon footprint of your food.

- Look for green hotels and B&Bs which make an effort to be environmentally friendly.

- Use your own toiletries to avoid the waste caused by discarded mini toiletries bottles.

- Only ask for room cleaning and laundry services for towels when absolutely necessary.

- Take a water bottle rather than relying on bottled water. Your hotel manager will be able to supply you with clean water.

- When leaving home, turn off all appliances and lower the thermostat.

- Use a carbon calculator to get an idea of what your vacation carbon footprint is. Then mitigate this carbon by buying carbon offset credits (they're much cheaper than you think.)

BRILLIANT CAMPING HACKS

• Use wire to attach a corks to your keys so they will float if you drop them in the drink.

• Use a large sealable plastic bag or put some air into the bag of wine you brought with you and use as a comfy pillow. Wine bags double as handy flotation devices.

• Frisbees: These offer amazing support for paper plates and make great water bowls for dogs.

• Wrap your headlamp around a clear water bottle to help diffuse the light in your tent.

• Tick Tac boxes: Great for storing spices and keeping matches dry. You can also dip the ends of your matches in wax or clear nail polish to make them waterproof.

• Pack pancake mix into sealable plastic bags. When you are ready to make them, add water, seal the bag and knead to mix. Then cut the bottom corner off the bag and pipe the mixture into your pan.

• Got a splinter? Place a small piece of banana peel onto the affected area and cover with a Band Aid. The splinter will dissolve after a day or two.

• Dirty plates or pots? Use sand to scour the worst of the dirt off and absorb the grease then rinse and wash.

• Need fire lighters? Doritos chips or crayons will burn for a couple of minutes which should be long enough to light your fire.

• Freeze water in water bottles to keep food cool over the first couple of days and for drinking towards the end of your trip.

• Substitute your tent pegs for solar lights to shed some light on your campsite and prevent tripping over tent ropes.

- Take out the inner cardboard tube from your toilet paper, squish it flat and keep in a sealable plastic bag to ensure that it stays dry.
- Making a cooking fire? You can make a ring of stones around the main fire and then a channel with parallel rows of stones coming off one side of your stone fire circle. This is your cooking area. Use a stick to scrape your coals over to the cooking area. This means you can continue to generate hot coals in your fire and move them over to the cooking area when you need them. This helps you to regulate the temperature and you won't get caught with a dying fire and an uncooked dinner.
- Relieve itchy mosquito bites with toothpaste.

BUG SPRAY

Make your own bug spray with natural ingredients.

WHAT YOU NEED	
I tbsp lemon eycalyptus oil	I tbsp. citronella oil
I tbsp. orange oil	I/2 cup witch hazel

INSTRUCTIONS

Mix ingredients in a spray bottle.

DON'T FORGET: OFFSET!

While you can move towards ensuring that the passage of your life doesn't leave the earth poorer for having provided you with a home, it's impossible to make no impact whatsoever. You don't have to have sleepless nights thinking about all the pollution and greenhouse gases you've produced when there are ways in which you can offset your footprint.

Neutralize the carbon you create with carbon offsets. These are credits (monetary donations) you give which go towards establishing wind farms and solar installations as well as energy-efficient retrofits. Use an online carbon calculator to calculate the emissions from your home, vehicle, air travel etc. and then search for carbon offset options in your area.

TIP Use cloth shopping bags rather than disposable plastic ones

TREE PLANTING

You can offset your carbon by planting trees in your neighborhood, in your yard, at local schools and other public places. If you live in an urban environment where this isn't possible, then search online for one of the many tree-planting organizations. These allow you to plant trees in your own country or restore jungles and forests in others.

If you planted a tree for every birthday, you would have created an entire forest by the time you died.

Forgo the cut tree at Christmas. Instead, buy a live tree in a pot (just think… no pesky needle cleanup!) and plant it in the spring. You get to enjoy the tree over the holidays and offset your carbon too.

It's not enough to simply reduce, you must renew too. With due diligence, you can restore, replenish and revitalize the earth's resources rather than depleting them over the course of your lifetime. That's a great legacy to leave.

NATURAL BURIALS: PUSHING UP DAISIES

You live sustainably, recycle and upcycle. Green living is your bag baby, but have you ever considered a green death? In the US alone, the two and half million people who die every year contribute significantly to greenhouse gas emissions and ground toxicity. But there is a more natural way to go. Many people choose to be cremated. Propane or natural gas make this process possible, but carbon dioxide gas is released. Burial is even harsher on the environment. Every year 827, 060 gallons of embalming fluid are buried in cemeteries in the US. Embalming fluid consists mostly of formaldehyde. More than 30-million board feet of hardwood is utilized in the making of coffins and every year, enough steel is buried to build another Golden Gate Bridge. Not to mention the copper and bronze or the carbon footprint of manufacturing and transporting coffins to the cemetery trailing a long line of mourners in their cars.

Cemeteries themselves require the clearing of natural habitats and the application of herbicides and pesticides to maintain the grounds. Garden and ground maintenance also releases greenhouse gases as most landscaping equipment still runs on gas.

More and more people are choosing a death that is sustainable and environmentally responsible. Depending on the area in which you live, there are now concessions for people who want these kinds of burials. Here bodies are wrapped in natural fiber shrouds or placed in biodegradable wicker or wood caskets. No embalming fluids or other chemicals are used on the body. The burial site is usually on private property (notice of the burial place must be given when the property is sold) in a natural habitat.

BUYING POWER

Be a conscious consumer by investigating where your products come from, their environmental impact and whether they are ethically manufactured. If some of your favorite brands have too much packaging or packaging that isn't biodegradable, write to them and ask for a more eco-friendly option. When consumers demand change, manufacturers will comply. Post on their social media sites so others can support your requests.

TIP Debunk the junk by saying no to community newspapers, political flyers and junk mail. Place a sign on your gate or mailbox which says no thank you to junk mail.

TIP If you feel strongly about a cause and have an overwhelming urge to fly a flag from your car window, think twice. A car sporting two window flags creates drag that costs an extra quart of fuel (0.94 liters) for each hour it travels at a speed of 65 mph (104 km/h). Opt for a bumper sticker, a t-shirt or lay the flag over your back seat.

TAKE UP A CAUSE

Find things that you are passionate about and join a movement to help preserve, save or clean up where you can. Of course you can donate, but you can also volunteer, sign petitions, write letters to your government representatives, join marches, raise funds and vote for leaders who are the best choice for the environment.

THANK YOUS

A lot of people worked really hard to make this book possible. I am so lucky and blessed to have you all in my life. Thank you all from the very bottom of my heart

The best mentor and friend a girl could ask for: David Shephard

The patient Zen master and design ninja: Benjamin Allison

Elvis reincarnate: Cornelius Quiring

Master craftsman: Igor Yu

Upcycling wizard: Ian Fotheringham

Beauty alchemist and ingenious imp: Mara Panacci

GREENMOXIE

Greenmoxie is your go-to spot for comprehensive ways to live sustainably. For everything on green living from ways to save energy and fuel, to toys you can make your kids from cardboard boxes, Greenmoxie has something for every situation and every family member. Learn how to make your own make up and beauty products (it's easier than you think) or find ways to winterize your home to save on heating costs; whatever you need, we have it for you. Learn to live a leaner, greener, healthier life that's sustainable, eco-friendly and saves you fistfullls of money! Living Greenmoxie is living right!

WWW.GREENMOXIE.COM

@GREENMOXIE

www.ingramcontent.com/pod-product-compliance
Lightning Source LLC
Chambersburg PA
CBHW052012030426
42334CB00029BA/3188